Hats
– a Knitter's dozen

a production of XRX BOOKS

Hats; A Knitter's dozen PUBLISHED BY XRX BOOKS

Credits

PUBLISHER
Alexis Yiorgos Xenakis

COEDITORS
Rick Mondragon
Elaine Rowley

EDITORIAL ASSISTANT
Sue Nelson

INSTRUCTION EDITOR
Joni Coniglio

INSTRUCTION ASSISTANTS
Cole Kelley
Ashley Mercer

GRAPHIC DESIGNER
Bob Natz

PHOTOGRAPHER
Alexis Xenakis

SECOND PHOTOGRAPHER
Mike Winkleman

DIRECTOR, PUBLISHING
SERVICES
David Xenakis

STYLIST
Rick Mondragon

TECHNICAL ILLUSTRATOR
Carol Skallerud

PRODUCTION DIRECTOR &
COLOR SPECIALIST
Dennis Pearson

BOOK PRODUCTION
MANAGER
Susan Becker

DIGITAL PREPRESS
Everett Baker
Nancy Holzer
Jay Reeve

MIS
Jason Bittner

FIRST PUBLISHED IN USA IN 2005 BY XRX, INC.

ISBN 1-933064-00-5
Produced in Sioux Falls, South Dakota, by XRX, Inc.,
PO Box 1525, Sioux Falls, SD 57101-1525 USA 605.338.2450

a publication of ✖◗✖ BOOKS

Visit us online at www.knittinguniverse.com

XRX BOOKS

Hats
– a Knitter's dozen

photography by
Alexis Xenakis

1

1 Shape 5 Finishes

2

Flip Your Lid

3

Chill Chaser

4

Pigtail Curls

5

Beach Beanies

6

Felted Four

12

Four Corners

13

Beaded Cloche

14

Snowbound Aran

15

Barber Pole Pair

16

Toe Hats

17

Fair Isle Friends

18

Nordkapp

19

Snowflakes

hats CONTENTS - a Knitter's dozen

Techniques
p 76

1 2 **3** 4 5 6

At a Glance
p 87

Specifications
p 86

Circular & 2-color
Knitting
p 84

Welcome

No matter what you call them—caps, bonnets, chapeaus, pillboxes, beanies, berets, tams, or cloches— hats are worn for many reasons. Wear them for warmth, style, status, communication, or just for fun.

And there are as many reasons to knit hats. Besides being great gifts, these small projects are portable and affordable. Combine colors of your favorite yarns. Better yet, get acquainted with something new—a hat only takes a ball or two. Try a variegated, mix stripes and textures, or make a 2-color stranded pattern.

It can be as easy as knitting a tube and sewing the top closed. Or just work decreases as the pattern says and go with the flow. Soon a shaped crown is complete, you've mastered working with circular needles, and double points dance in your hands.

You can audition other techniques you might not tackle on a larger scale. Sample short rows, miters, felting, and weaving; maybe you'll choose to add beads, sock toes, or I-cord accents.

So, let the fun begin. Soon you'll find the yarn racing through your fingers and onto your head.

This is the perfect project for teaching children to knit. The knitting itself is basic, there is no shaping, and the kids end up with something they can actually use! Choose from five finishing options to customize the hat to your taste. This pattern will give the beginner the opportunity to practice casting on, knitting, purling, ribbing, binding off, and sewing.

Designed by Maureen Egan Emlet

1 Shape, 5 Finishes

it's easy ...go for it!

EASY

Child S (M, L, 1X)
Circumference 18 (19, 21, 22½)"
Length 7 (7¾, 8½, 9)"

10cm/4"

26
17

• over stockinette stitch (knit on RS, purl on WS) using larger needles

1 2 3 **4** 5 6

• Medium weight
HATS • A, B, C, D
MC • 178 yds
CC • 20 yds
HAT • E
MC • 178 yds
CC1 & CC2 • 15 yds each

• 3.5mm/US4 and 5mm/US8
or size to obtain gauge

&

• yarn needle, stitch markers (Hat E),
2 decorative buttons (Hat B)

Note

See *Techniques*, page 76, for making pompons and tassels.

ALL HATS

With smaller needles and MC, cast on 76 (82, 90, 96) stitches. Work 1" in k1, p1 rib. Change to larger needles. Work in stockinette stitch until piece measures 7 (7¾, 8½, 9)" from beginning.

HAT A

Bind off all stitches. Sew back seam. Fold hat so that seam is at center back (figure 1). Sew top seam straight across (figure 2).

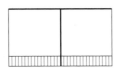

figure 1   figure 2

Tassels

With CC, make two 4" tassels and attach one to each top corner.

Hat A CARON *Wintuk Solid Colors (acrylic; 100g; 213 yds) in 3031 Navy (MC) and Ombre (acrylic; 84g; 178 yds) in 3613 Night Skies (CC)*

HAT B

Work as for Hat A. Fold top corners down to 2¼ (2½, 2¾, 3)" above cast-on row (figure 3). Sew in place with button over point.

figure 3

Hat B CARON Wintuk Ombre (acrylic; 84g; 178 yds) in 3613 Night Skies

HAT C

Do not bind off stitches. Cut yarn, leaving a 12" tail. Thread tail through live stitches, then sew back seam (figure 4). Pull tail snugly, gathering stitches to close the top (figure 5). Sew a few stitches to secure the top.

Pompons

With 1 strand each of MC and CC, make a 2½" pompon and attach to top of hat.

Hat C CARON Wintuk Solid Colors (acrylic; 100g; 213 yds) in 3254 Sky Blue (MC) and 3002 Off-white (CC)

figure 4

figure 5

3

Hat D CARON *Wintuk Solid Colors (acrylic; 100g; 213 yds) in 3255 Periwinkle*

HAT D

Work as for Hat A. Fold top corners up to meet at center seam (figure 6). Sew corners in place.

Bobble

With larger needles, cast on 1 stitch.

Row 1 K1.

Row 2 Knit into front and back of stitch until there are 7 stitches total.

Rows 3–8 Knit.

Row 9 K7. Pass first 6 stitches, one at a time, over last stitch and off needle. Fasten off, leaving 4" tail. Using tails, sew bobble to top of hat where points meet.

figure 6

HAT E

Bind off all stitches. Sew back seam. Beginning at seam, place 4 markers evenly around top edge (figure 7). With WS together, fold hat, matching markers 1 & 2. Sew seam. Repeat, matching markers 2 & 3, 3 & 4, then 4 & 1 (figure 8).

Pompons

Make two 2" pompons, each with CC1 and CC2. Attach 1 to each corner.

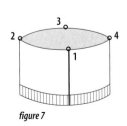

figure 7

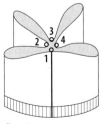

figure 8

Hat E CARON *Wintuk Solid Colors (acrylic; 100g; 213 yds) in 3002 Off-white (MC), 3255 Periwinkle (CC1), and 3031 Navy (CC2)*

4

2

EASY +

S (M, L)
Circumference 19½ (21¾, 23)"

10cm/4"

27

18

• over stockinette stitch (knit every round)

1 2 3 **4** 5 6

• Medium weight
• 120 (150, 180) yds

• 4.5mm/US7, or size to obtain gauge,
40cm/16" long

• five size 4.5mm/US7

• eight 15mm/⅝" blue round
• eight 12mm/½" white star-shaped
• one 24mm/1" white star-shaped

• 5.5mm/I

&

• stitch marker

Colorful and funky, this "Jughead" hat is meant to be fun. Pick a variegated cotton yarn that you love and a few great buttons for a cool look. This hat will bring smiles to everyone.

Designed by Betty Monroe

Flip Your Lid

Notes
1 See *Techniques*, page 76, for SSK, SK2P, and crochet cast-on. **2** Work hat with circular needle, changing to double-pointed needles when necessary. **3** Work body of hat first, then pick up and knit stitches for scalloped band along crochet cast-on.

HAT
With crochet cast-on, cast on 85 (97, 109) stitches. Place marker (pm) and join, being careful not to twist stitches.
Begin Rib Pattern: Round 1 * K1, p1; repeat from * to last stitch, slip (sl) last stitch to right needle, remove marker, sl stitch back to left needle, replace marker.
Round 2 K2tog, * p1, k1; repeat from *, end p1—84 (96, 108) stitches.
Rounds 3–5 * K1, p1; repeat from * to end.
Rounds 6–9 Knit.
Next round [K1, SSK, k8 (10, 12), SSK, k1] 6 times—72 (84, 96) stitches.
Knit 15 (15, 21) rounds (or desired length to crown shaping). Piece measures approximately 4 (4, 5)" from beginning.

Shape crown
Round 1 [K1, SSK, k6 (8, 10), SSK, k1] 6 times—60 (72, 84) stitches.

Rounds 2–4 Knit.
Round 5 [K1, SSK, k4 (6, 8), SSK, k1] 6 times—48 (60, 72) stitches.
Rounds 6–7 Knit.
Round 8 [K1, SSK, k2 (4, 6), SSK, k1] 6 times—36 (48, 60) stitches.
Round 9 Knit.
Round 10 [K1, SK2P, k2 (4, 6)] 6 times—24 (36, 48) stitches.
Round 11 Knit.
Round 12 [K1, SK2P, k0 (2, 4)] 6 times—12 (24, 36) stitches.
Round 13 Knit.
SIZE L ONLY: **Round 14** [K1, SK2P, k2] 6 times—24 stitches.
Round 15 Knit.
ALL SIZES: **Next round** [K2tog] 6 (12, 12) times—6 (12, 12) stitches. Cut yarn, leaving an approximately 6" long tail. Run yarn through all stitches twice and pull to tighten.

Scalloped band
Turn hat so that purl side is facing outside (now the RS of work). With RS facing, pick up and knit 84 (96, 108) stitches along crochet cast-on, picking up 1 stitch under each link of chain (see illustration on next page).

LION BRAND Lion Cotton (cotton; 113g; 189 yds) in 208 Wedgewood

Pm, join and work in rounds as follows:
Next round Purl, increase 4 (0, decrease 4) stitches evenly around—88 (96, 104) stitches.
Next 3 rounds Purl.
Next round [P11 (12, 13), pm] 7 times, p11 (12, 13).
Next round Purl to marker, turn work. Begin working back and forth in rows over these 11 (12, 13) stitches as follows (do not wrap stitches at turns):
* **Row 1** (RS) K10 (11, 12), turn, leaving remaining stitch unworked.
Row 2 P9 (10, 11), turn.
Row 3 K8 (9, 10), turn.
Row 4 P7 (8, 9), turn.
Row 5 K6 (7, 8), turn.
Row 6 P5 (6, 7), turn.
Row 7 K4 (5, 6), turn.
Row 8 P3 (4, 5), turn.
Row 9 K2 (3, 4), turn.
Row 10 P0 (2, 3), turn.
Row 11 K0 (1, 2), turn.
Next row Purl to next marker.
Repeat from * 7 times more (8 scallops created). Bind off all stitches knitwise. Fold band up so that knit side of band is facing out. Sew 2 buttons on each point of scallop, with a blue button on the bottom and a star button on top, sewing through both band and cap to keep band in place. Sew large star button to top of hat.

3

Here's another inventive, simple design that makes a great gift. This convertible cap/cowl will keep you warm in all kinds of weather. The 2x2 ribbed tube, knit in a pleasing variegated yarn, has a drawstring at one end. Tie it for a hat, or leave it open and pull the tube down around your neck.

Designed by Julie Gaddy

Chill Chasers

it's easy
...go for it!

Notes
See *Techniques*, page 76, for yarn-over (yo) before a knit and purl stitch and twisted cord.

CAP/COWL
Cast on 96 stitches. Place marker and join, being careful not to twist stitches.
Begin K2, P2 rib: Round 1 * K2, p2; repeat from * around. Repeat Round 1 until piece measures 10".
Eyelet round * K2tog, yo, p2tog, yo; repeat from * around. Work 2 rounds more in k2, p2 rib. Bind off in rib pattern.

Finishing
Block piece. Add drawstring.
Drawstring
With 3 strands of yarn, make a 12" twisted cord. Weave through eyelets.

EASY

Circumference 19"
Length 10½"

10cm/4"
18
20
• over k2, p2 rib

1 2 3 4 **5** 6
• Bulky weight
• 220 yds

• 6.5mm/US10½
or size to obtain gauge,
40cm/16" long

&
• stitch marker

MUENCH YARNS *Naturwolle (wool; 100g; 110 yds)* in Kunterbunt

Hand-dyed colors and playful shaping combine in a cheery hat. The flaps will warm your ears, and the squared top and crochet trim "pigtails" will bring a smile to everyone around you!

Designed by Angela Juergens

Pigtail Curls

EASY +

One size
Circumference 19"

10cm/4"

28

14

• over seed stitch with 3 strands A and 1
strand B held together

1 2 3 4 5 6

• Superfine weight
A • 450 yds
B • 150 yds

• 6.5mm/US10½,
or size to obtain gauge
40cm/16" long

• 3.25mm/D

&

• stitch marker

Notes
1 See *Techniques*, page 76, for crochet chain stitch (ch st), single crochet (sc) and backward single crochet. **2** Work with 3 strands A and 1 strand B held together, unless otherwise indicated. **3** Hat is worked circularly from crown to beginning of flap, then worked back and forth in rows. **4** For ease in working, mark RS of work.

Seed Stitch (over an odd number of stitches)
Row 1 K1, * p1, k1; repeat from *.
Row 2 Knit the purl stitches and purl the knit stitches. Repeat Row 2 for Seed Stitch.

HAT
Cast on 67 stitches. Place marker and join, being careful not to twist stitches. Work Seed Stitch for 45 rounds.

Flap shaping
Next round Work 27 stitches, loosely bind off 13 stitches (front opening), work to end of round, then remove marker and work next 27 stitches, ending at bound-off stitches. Turn work. Work back and forth in rows on 54 stitches, beginning with a WS row. Bind off 2 stitches at beginning of

next 2 rows, 1 stitch at beginning of next 2 rows—48 stitches. ***Next row*** (WS) Work 22 stitches, loosely bind off 4 stitches (back opening), work to end.

Left flap
Work over 22 stitches as follows:
Row 1 (RS) Bind off 1 stitch, work to end.
Row 2 Bind off 4 stitches, work to end.
Row 3 Work even.
Rows 4, 6, and 8 Bind off 2 stitches, work to end.
Rows 5, 7, 9, and 10 Bind off 1 stitch, work to end—7 stitches. Work 22 rows even. Bind off.

Right flap
Join yarn at front edge of right flap, ready to work a WS row. Work Rows 1–10 as for left flap, working odd-numbered rows on WS. Work 21 rows even. Bind off remaining 7 stitches.

Finishing
With 1 strand A and B held together, work backward sc around lower edge of hat. Sew seam at top of hat. Iron hat on highest setting, putting a wet towel between iron and hat.

KOIGU KPPPM (wool; 50g; 175 yds) in P114 Multi (A) and KPM (wool; 50g; 175 yds) in 2229 Red (B)

Tassel (make 2)

With 1 strand A and B held together, * loosely ch 21 stitches, work sc tightly in 2nd ch st from hook, then in every stitch to end (working sc tightly will make the chain curl), then without breaking yarn, loosely ch 31 stitches, work sc tightly in 2nd ch from hook, then in every stitch to end; repeat from * twice more, then ch 21 and work sc as before—7 fringes. Sew one tassel to each top corner of hat.

5

Requiring less than 150 yards of yarn, this beanie pattern is so easy that you can complete one in an evening or two. It's a great way to use up those leftover skeins and make a matching accessory or a great gift.

Designed by Maggie DeCuir

Beach Beanies

it's easy ...go for it!

EASY +

One size
Circumference 20"

10cm/4"

40
19

• over Eyelet Pattern

1 2 **3** 4 5 6

• Light weight
• 110 yds

• 4mm/US6, or size to obtain gauge
40cm/16" long

• four 4mm/US6

&

• stitch marker

12

Notes
1 See *Techniques*, page 76, for yarn over (yo). **2** Work with circular needle, changing to double-pointed needles when there are too few stitches to fit on circular needle.

Eyelet Pattern (over a multiple of 4 stitches)
Round 1 * K2, yo, k2tog; repeat from *.
Round 2 and all even-numbered rounds Knit.
Round 3 K1, * k2, yo, k2tog; repeat from *, end k3.
Round 5 Yo, k2tog, * k2, yo, k2tog; repeat from *, end k2.
Round 7 K1, yo, k2tog, * k2, yo, k2tog; repeat from *, end k1.
Round 8 Knit. Repeat Rounds 1–8 for Eyelet Pattern.

BEANIE
Cast on 96 stitches. Place marker, join, being careful not to twist stitches. Work in rounds as follows: [Knit 1 round, purl 1 round] 4 times. Work Eyelet Pattern until piece measures 4" from beginning.

Shape crown
Round 1 * K6, k2tog; repeat from *.
Round 2 and all even-numbered rounds Knit.
Round 3 * K5, k2tog; repeat from *.
Round 5 * K4, k2tog; repeat from *.
Round 7 * K3, k2tog; repeat from *.
Round 9 * K2, k2tog; repeat from *.
Round 11 * K1, k2tog; repeat from *.
Rounds 13 and 15 * K2tog; repeat from *.
Cut yarn and draw through remaining 6 stitches and pull together. Secure yarn to WS.

CLASSIC ELITE *Imagine (cotton and rayon; 50g; 93 yds) in 9201 Bleach*

PATONS Cotton DK (cotton; 100g;
230 yds) in 6313 Hyacinth Purple

Here we give you felting with four different looks and styles. So whether you are looking for a toned-down classic, a colorful cloche, or a casual earflap cap–try one of these. The yarns are the perfect felting fibers: wools or wool blends.

Designed by Susan Guagliumi and Rachel Nash Law

The Felted Four

INTERMEDIATE

One size to fit average adult

10cm/4"

BERET (HAT)
24 (22)

18 (12)

• before felting, over stockinette stitch
(use double strand for Hat)

1 2 3 **4** 5 6

• Medium weight
BERET & HAT • 225 yds each

BERET • 4.5mm/US7, or size to obtain gauge
HAT • 5.5mm/US9, or size to obtain gauge

BERET • two 4.5mm/US7

&

• stitch holder (Beret)
• grosgrain ribbon (Hat)
• waste yarn & ravel cord

Note

See *Techniques,* page 76, for wrapping stitches on short rows, invisible cast-on, grafting, and I-cord.

Felting Instructions for all hats

Soak hat in hot water for 10 minutes so fibers are saturated and open. Place hat in zippered pillow case and put in washing machine with towels. Add detergent and set washer for hot wash, cold rinse. Check every 4–5 minutes until hat is felted as desired. Let washer spin only briefly between cycles to avoid creases. Pat into shape; lay flat to dry (Beret) or block over round shape (Hats).

BERET

Cast on 45 stitches, using invisible cast-on.
Begin short-row shaping:
Row 1 (RS) Slip (sl) 1, knit to end.
Row 2 P41, wrap stitch and turn (W&T).
Row 3 Knit.
Row 4 P37, W&T.
Row 5 K20, W&T.
Row 6 P16, W&T.
Row 7 K20, W&T.
Rows 8–11 Repeat Rows 6-7 twice.
Row 12 P15, W&T.
Row 13 K17, W&T.

Row 14 P22, W&T.
Row 15 K16, W&T.
Row 16 P20, W&T.
Row 17 K16, W&T.
Rows 18–19 Repeat Rows 16–17 once.
Row 20 P20, W&T.
Row 21 K37.
Row 22 P41, W&T.
Row 23 K41.
Row 24 P44, W&T.
Row 25 K44.
Row 26 Purl all stitches. Repeat Rows 1–26 for 8 times more, then Rows 1–24 once. Place 45 stitches on hold. With WS facing and double-pointed needle (dpn), pick up and knit 3 stitches from center of crown. Work 10 rounds of I-cord.

Finishing

Graft 45 stitches on holder to 45 cast-on stitches. Use yarn tail to close up center of crown. Felt as instructed above.

ROLLED-BRIM HAT
Notes

1 See *Techniques*, page 76, for wrapping stitches on short rows, invisible cast-on, and grafting. ***2*** Use double-strand of yarn throughout.

Beret PLYMOUTH *Galway (wool; 100g; 230 yds) in 31 Teal* **Rolled-brim hat** *in 13 Purple*

Hat

With double-strand of purple cast on 39 stitches, using invisible cast-on. *Begin short-row shaping: Row 1* (RS) P17, turn. *Row 2* Slip (sl) 1, k16. *Row 3* P36, turn.
Row 4 Sl 1, k35. *Row 5* P34, turn.
Row 6 Sl 1, k21, turn. *Row 7* Sl 1, p19, turn. *Row 8* Sl 1, k31.
Row 9 P30, turn. *Row 10* Sl 1, k29.
Row 11 P17, turn. *Row 12* Sl 1, k16.
Row 13 P30, wrap stitch and turn (W&T).
Row 14 K30. *Row 15* P32, W&T. *Row 16* K20, turn. *Row 17* Sl 1, p21, W&T. *Row 18* K34. *Row 19* P36, W&T. *Row 20* K36.
Row 21 P17, turn. *Row 22* Sl 1, k16. *Row 23* P39.

Row 24 K39. Repeat Rows 1–24 for 7 times more, then Rows 1–23 once.

Finishing

Graft last 39 stitches to 39 cast-on stitches. Work in all ends, gathering top of crown slightly if necessary to close hole. Pull fabric lengthwise to align stitches. Felt as instructed on page 14.
When dry, sew grosgrain ribbon around inside to maintain fit.

15

One size to fit average adult

10cm/4"

20 (24)

13 (13)
• before felting (after felting), over
stockinette stitch (knit every round)

1 2 3 **4** 5 6

• Medium weight
CLOCHE • 250 yds
EARFLAP HAT • MC • 125 yds
• CC • 50 yds each of 3 colors

• 6.5mm/US10½, or size to obtain gauge,
60cm/24" long

• four 6.5mm/US10½

&

• stitch markers

CLOCHE
Notes
1 See *Techniques,* page 76, for SSK
and twisted cord. *2* Change to double-
pointed needles (dpn) when necessary.

Brim
With circular needle, cast on 96 stitches.
Place marker and join, being careful not
to twist stitches. Knit 3 rounds.

Make brim ridge
Turn knitting inside out with purl side
on the outside.

Next round Slip (sl) 1 stitch from right
needle to left needle, bring yarn to front
and sl same stitch back to right needle
(one stitch wrapped). Knit 1 round to
wrapped stitch, knit wrap and stitch
together (hiding wrap). Knit until piece
measures 3½" from beginning.

Decrease round * K2, k2tog; repeat from *
—72 stitches.

Eyelet round * K2, SSK, yo; repeat from *.
Knit every round until piece measures
5" above eyelet round.

Shape crown
Decrease round 1 [K6, k2tog] 9 times—
63 stitches.

Round 2 and all even-numbered rounds Knit.

Round 3 [K5, k2tog] 9 times—54 stitches.
Continue in this way to decrease 9

CLASSIC ELITE *Montera (llama, wool; 100g; 127
yds) in 3872 Teal*

stitches (working 1 less knit stitch
between decreases) every other round
until 9 stitches remain.

Next round [K2tog] 4 times, k1—5
stitches. Cut yarn, draw through stitches
tightly and fasten off.

Finishing
Thread non-wool yarn through eyelets and
tie securely.
Felt as instructed on page 14.
Remove non-wool yarn from eyelets. Cut 1
length of teal yarn approximately 6 yards
long and make a twisted cord. Thread
cord through eyelets.

Chart pattern

19

10

1

4-st repeat

■ Black
□ Yellow green
□ Gold
▨ Orange

CLASSIC ELITE Montera (llama, wool; 100g; 127 yds) in 3813 Black, 3881 Yellow green, 3898 Gold, and 3868 Orange

EARFLAP HAT

Notes
1 See *Techniques,* page 76, for SSK, SSP, and twisted cord. **2** For ease in working, use different-colored stitch markers when marking position of earflaps. **3** Strand yarns loosely when working Chart pattern as stranded knitting felts more quickly than plain stockinette stitch. **4** Change to double-pointed needles when necessary.

Hat
With circular needle and black, cast on 76 stitches. Place marker (pm), join, being careful not to twist stitches: Knit 1 round, placing markers for earflaps as follows: between stitches 3 & 4, 35 & 36, 49 & 50, and 65 & 66 (leave these markers on first row). Place another marker between stitches 38 & 39 to mark

halfway point. Work 19 rounds in Chart pattern, then work even in stockinette stitch with black until piece measures 6" from beginning.

Shape front crown
Begin at round marker, knit to marker at halfway point. Turn, purl to round marker. Turn, knit to 8 stitches before halfway marker. Turn, purl to 8 stitches before round marker. Turn. Knit 2 rounds, ending at round marker.

Shape crown
Decrease round 1 [K5, k2tog] 10 times, k6—66 stitches.
Round 2 and all even-numbered rounds Knit.
Round 3 [K4, k2tog] 11 times—55 stitches.
Round 5 [K3, k2tog] 11 times—44 stitches. Continue in this way to decrease 11 stitches (working 1 less knit stitch between decreases) every other round until 11 stitches remain.
Next round [K2tog] 5 times, k1—6 stitches. Cut yarn, draw through stitches tightly and fasten off.

Earflaps (make 2)
With RS facing and black, pick up and knit 14 stitches between markers at lower edge of hat: For first flap, pick up stitches between markers at stitches 3 & 4 and 65 & 66; for 2nd flap, pick up stitches between markers at stitches 35 & 36 and 49 & 50. Work 11 rows in stockinette stitch, end with a WS row.
Next row (RS) K1, k2tog, knit to last 3 stitches, SSK, k1.
Next row P1, SSP, purl to last 3 stitches, p2tog, p1. Repeat last 2 rows until 2 stitches remain. Bind off.

Finishing
Felt as instructed on page 14.
Cut 2 lengths of black approximately 3 yards long and make twisted cords. Attach one to each earflap.

7

Making accessories year round is an excellent way to keep up with your gift-giving plans. Here's a hat that's uncomplicated and a pleasure to knit, and because of the cozy acrylic chenille, it can be a trans-seasonal topper or worn by someone who simply needs a soft head covering.

Designed by Jean Inda

Chenille Chapeau

Notes
1 Work with 2 strands of yarn held together throughout. **2** Change to double-pointed needles when necessary.

HAT
With circular needle and 2 strands of yarn, cast on 90 stitches. Place marker and join, being careful not to twist stitches. Knit 4 rounds. * Purl 1 round. Knit 1 round. Repeat from * until piece measures 4" from beginning, end with a purl round.
Next round * K2tog, k1; repeat from * around—60 stitches.
Next round * K1, p1; repeat from * around. Repeat last round for 1". Knit every round for 3½".

Shape top
Round 1 and all odd-numbered rounds Purl.
Round 2 [K4, k2tog] 10 times—50 stitches.
Round 4 [K3, k2tog] 10 times—40 stitches.
Round 6 [K2, k2tog] 10 times—30 stitches.
Round 8 [K1, k2tog] 10 times—20 stitches.
Round 10 [K2tog] 10 times—10 stitches.
Round 11 Purl.

Cut yarn, leaving an 8" tail. Run yarn through remaining stitches and pull together tightly. Fasten off.

Finishing
Weave a strand of yarn on the inside through center of k1, p1 rib, and tie in a bow. Adjust hat as needed. Turn up brim.

SPINRITE Chenille (acrylic; 40g; 85 yds) in 6302 Oatmeal

There's a knitting workshop in this neat little package, providing skill-building lessons on a small scale. This unique piece includes a rolled brim, woven stitch body and rounded crown with I-cord topping.

Designed by Susan Douglas

Woven Chapeau

EASY+
One size
Circumference 21"

10cm/4"

40
20

• over garter stitch
(knit 1 round, purl 1 round)
using larger needles and MC

1 2 **3** 4 5 6

• Light weight
• MC 175 yds
• CC 50 yds

• 3.5mm/US4 and 4mm/US6, or size to
obtain gauge, 60cm/24" long

• four 4mm/US6
• one 3.5mm/US4

• 3.75mm/G

• stitch marker
• yarn needle
• fiber fill

Notes
1 See *Techniques*, page 76, for SSK, chain cast-on and unattached I-cord. *2* Change to dpns when necessary.

Rolled brim
With smaller needle and CC, cast on 132 stitches, using chain cast-on. Place marker and join, being careful not to twist stitches. Knit 23 rounds.
Joining round (Stuff brim as you work joining round.) Bring cast-on edge up in front of needle so purl side faces out, then work as follows: * Place 15–20 cast-on stitches onto smaller double-pointed needle (dpn), unravelling chain, then knit 1 stitch from dpn together with 1 stitch from needle until these 15–20 stitches are worked; repeat from * around. Knit 1 round.

Body
Change to larger circular needle and MC. **Next round** * [K2, k2tog] twice, k1, k2tog; repeat from *—96 stitches. [Purl 1 round, knit 1 round] 13 times, purl 1 round.

Top ridge
With CC, knit 1 round. Purl 9 rounds. Change to MC.
Shape crown
Note
Rounds 1 and 2 Knit.
Round 3 [K6, k2tog, SSK, k6] 6 times.
Rounds 4-6 Knit.
Round 7 [K5, k2tog, SSK, k5] 6 times.
Rounds 8–10 Knit.
Round 11 [K4, k2tog, SSK, k4] 6 times.
Rounds 12–14 Knit.
Round 15 [K3, k2tog, SSK, k3] 6 times.
Rounds 16, 18 , and 20 Knit.
Round 17 [K2, k2tog, SSK, k2] 6 times.
Round 19 [K1, k2tog, SSK, k1] 6 times.
Round 21 [K2tog, SSK] 6 times.
Round 22 [K2tog] 6 times. Place remaining 6 stitches on one dpn. With CC, work unattached I-cord for 20 rounds. Break yarn, run tail through stitches, tighten and secure. Tie cord into a knot.

Finishing
Turn hat inside out and with yarn needle and CC, whip stitch upper and lower CC loops of top ridge together to form welt on RS. With MC, weave stitches of garter stitch portion of hat (see next page).

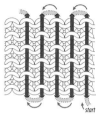

Surface weaving

If you examine the garter stitch portion of the hat, you will notice "up bumps" in the stitches. Using a yarn needle and a separate strand of the main-color yarn, begin at the bottom of the section and bring the yarn alternately over and under the "up bumps" in one vertical column of stitches. When you reach the top, take the yarn down through to the wrong side of the work. Bring the yarn up to the right side again above the next column to the left and weave down. Keep the tension even, adjusting the weaving yarn as the work progresses.

K1, C2 Parfait Swirls (wool; 50g; 100 yds) in 4999 Licorice (MC) and Creme Brulee DK (wool; 50g; 131 yds) in 905 Charcoal (CC)

9

Wrapping fabric around one's head is a part of many native costumes, and even contemporary adornments. This wrap-and-twist hat is an unusual and clever take on a winter topper: a triangle is folded in sections that spiral around. The simple stitch pattern and easy crochet finishing will have you covered in no time.

Designed by Annie Modesitt

Triangle Hat

it's easy
...go for it!

EASY +

S (M , L)
Circumference
20 (21½, 23)"

10cm/4"

26
18

• over Garter Rib Stripe pattern

1 2 3 **4** 5 6

• Medium weight
A • 90 yds each size
B • 70 yds each size
C • 70 yds each size

• 5mm/US8, or size to obtain gauge

• 4mm/G

Notes
1 See *Techniques*, page 76, for single crochet (sc), tassels, and twisted cord.
2 Carry yarn loosely along side of work until needed.

Garter Rib pattern (over an odd number of stitches)
Row 1 (RS) Knit.
Row 2 * K1, p1; repeat from *, end k1. Repeat Rows 1 and 2 for Garter Rib pattern.

Garter Rib Stripe pattern
Repeat Rows 1 and 2 of Garter Rib pattern, working in Stripe pattern as follows: * 4 rows B, 2 rows A, 4 rows C, 2 rows A; repeat from *.

Decrease Row
(WS) K1, p2tog, work in established pattern to end. (***Note*** Begin all unshaped WS rows with k1, p1, then work in established pattern to end.)

HAT
With A, cast on 49 (57, 61) stitches.
Begin Rib: Row 1 (RS) * P1, k1; repeat from *, end p1.
Row 2 * K1, p1; repeat from *, end k1.
Repeat Rows 1 and 2 twice more.
Work Garter Rib Stripe Pattern and shaping as follows: [Work 3 rows even in pattern, work Decrease Row on next row, work 1 row even, work Decrease Row on next row] 23 (27, 25) times—3 (3, 11) stitches.
SIZE L ONLY Work Decrease Row every 4th row 7 times, work 1 row even, work Decrease Row once more—3 stitches.
ALL SIZES K3tog. Fasten off last stitch. Piece measures approximately 22 (26, 28½)" from beginning.

Finishing
Block piece. Place a safety pin on slanted edge 6 (7, 7¾)" down from tip of hat. With WS together, fold hat at pin (Point B) so that tip of triangle (Point A) meets Point C (Step 1). With crochet hook and A, join seam with sc worked through both thicknesses (removing pin). Continue folding hat and crocheting edges as shown

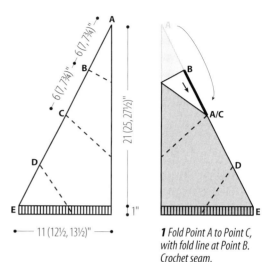

□ RS
▨ WS
- - - - - Fold line
━━━➤ Direction of crocheted seam

1 Fold Point A to Point C, with fold line at Point B. Crochet seam.

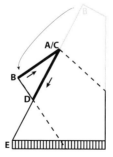

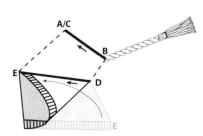

2 Fold at Point C so that fold-line B meets Point D. Crochet seam.

3 Fold at Point D so that fold-line C meets Point E. Crochet seam.

CHERRY TREE HILL YARNS *Cotton Boucle Mini (cotton; 125g; 170 yds) in Loden (A); BROWN SHEEP Lamb's Pride (wool, mohair; 125g; 190 yds) in Multi (B) and Purple (C)*

in folding diagrams. After Step 3 is complete, continue working sc along edge of hat, ending at lower edge of ribbing.

With yarn A, make a 5" tassel and a 5" twisted cord. Attach knotted end of twisted cord to top corner of hat, then attach tassel to other end of cord.

10

Choose a great yarn and you cannot go wrong. When I first saw Horst Schulz's work, I thought it'd be fun to make a simple hat. As I worked, I kept thinking that shaping the diamonds would present interesting design opportunities. The concept I followed is simple. An added decrease in the upper level squares would shrink the diamonds in size, and shape the crown of the hat. It worked!

Designed by David Xenakis

Diamond Head

INTERMEDIATE

M (L)
Circumference 21 (24)"

• 1 square (Chart A) = 3", measured on the diagonal (along center decreases)

1 2 3 **4** 5 6

• Medium weight
• 330 yds each size

• 3.5mm/US4, or size to obtain gauge

Notes

1 See *Techniques*, page 76, for SSK, SSP, loop cast-on, pick up and knit, and I-cord. *2* Use loop cast-on throughout.

1st tier of 7 (8) squares

Cast on 22 stitches. Work 20 rows of Chart A. Break yarn and place last 2 stitches on hold (Photo 1).

2nd tier of squares

With RS of one square facing, begin at left of stitches on hold and pick up and knit 10 stitches down left edge of square, cast on 2 stitches, then pick up and knit 10 stitches along right edge of a 2nd square, end at right of stitches on hold (Photo 2)—22 stitches. * Work 20 rows of Chart A. Break yarn and place last 2 stitches on hold (Photo 3). Pick up along left edge of last joined square from 1st tier, cast on 2 stitches, then pick up and knit 10 stitches along right edge of another square from 1st tier. Repeat from *, joining 7th (8th) square to first square of previous tier, forming a circle.

3rd tier of squares

Work as for 2nd tier of squares, except knit 2 stitches from holder instead of casting on.

Chart A

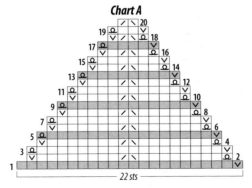

— 22 sts —

☐ K on RS, p on WS
▨ K on WS
╱ K2tog on RS, p2tog on WS
╲ SSK on RS, SSP on WS
ⴸ Sl 1 purlwise with yarn in front
ⵕ K1 through back loop (tbl)

Photo 1

Photo 2

Photo 3

Photo 4

1 One finished square from 1st tier.
2 Joining squares of 1st tier and picking up stitches for 2nd tier.
3 Completed square from 2nd tier.
4 Completed half square from lower edge.

L NORO Kureyon (wool; 50g; 110 yds) in 126

25

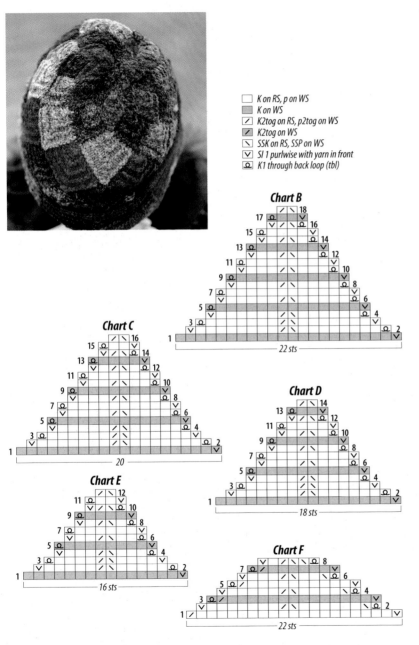

Legend:
- ☐ K on RS, p on WS
- ▨ K on WS
- ╱ K2tog on RS, p2tog on WS
- ╱ K2tog on WS
- ╲ SSK on RS, SSP on WS
- ⌄ Sl 1 purlwise with yarn in front
- ⚲ K1 through back loop (tbl)

Chart B
(22 sts)

Chart C
(20)

Chart D
(18 sts)

Chart E
(16 sts)

Chart F
(22 sts)

4th tier of squares

Pick up and knit stitches as for 3rd tier. Work 18 rows of Chart B. Place remaining 2 stitches on hold.

5th tier of squares

Pick up stitches as before, except pick up 9 stitches, instead of 10, along sides of squares—20 stitches. Work 16 rows of Chart C.

6th tier of squares

Pick up 8 stitches along sides of squares—18 stitches. Work 14 rows of Chart D.

7th tier of squares

Pick up 7 stitches along sides of squares—16 stitches. Work 12 rows of Chart E.

Finish the top

Turn hat inside out, take the final stitches and loop one stitch over the next around to resemble a bound-off row. Take final stitch and pull tail through, around first, and back to finish the bind-off. Take each tail and seam each little section, between squares, sewing in one full stitch.

Half square lower edge

Turn hat upside down and with RS facing, pick up and knit stitches along original cast-on edge as before, picking up 10 stitches along sides of squares and 2 in the center—22 stitches (Photo 4 on page 25). Work 8 rows of Chart F. Bind off remaining 6 stitches.

Hat band

With WS facing, begin at center of a half square and pick up and knit 16 stitches to center of next square. Purl 1 row. * Knit 3 rows. Purl 1 row. Repeat from * four times more. Turn work. Cast on 3 stitches onto left needle and work I-cord bind-off as follows: * K2, k2tog through the back loop, slip stitches back to left needle; repeat from * across. Place stitches on holder. Break yarn leaving 8″ tail. Work next 16-stitch section as before, except don't cast on for I-cord, use the stitches from holder. Repeat sections around, grafting final I-cord edge to its beginning. Use tails to seam sections of band. Block to size required.

M *NORO Kureyon (wool; 50g; 110 yds) in Mardigras*

Here's a whimsical and warm hat that looks like a miniature Aran sweater for your head! Have fun with the sleeves—wear them fore and aft, port and starboard, or tied on top of your head. Double the ribbing for warmth, as shown here, or leave it as a single layer. Omit the sleeves and neckband for a squared-off Aran cap.

Designed by Gayle Roehm

Sweaters on your Head

INTERMEDIATE

Sizes XS (S, M, L, 1X)
Circumference 17 (18½, 20½, 22, 23½)"

10cm/4"

24

20

• over Moss stitch, using larger needles

1 2 3 **4** 5 6

• Medium weight
• 300 yds each hat

• 3.5mm/US4 and 4mm/US6, or size to obtain gauge, 40cm/16" long

• four each size 3.5mm/US4 and 4mm/US6

<del>⌐⌐⌐</del>

• 3.5mm/E

&

• stitch markers and holders
• cable needle (cn)

Notes
1 See *Techniques,* page 76, for chain cast-on, S2KP2, and 3-needle bind-off.
2 Work hat circularly through round 26 of Chart B (on page 30), then divide and work front and back separately back and forth in rows.

Twisted Rib (over an even number of stitches)
Round 1 * K1 through back loop (tbl), p1; repeat from *.
Repeat Round 1 for Twisted Rib.

Moss stitch (over an even number of stitches)
Rounds (or Rows) 1 and 2 * K1, p1; repeat from *.
Rounds (or Rows) 3 and 4 * P1, k1; repeat from *. Repeat Rounds (or Rows) 1–4 for Moss stitch.

LION BRAND Wool-Ease (acrylic, wool; 85g; 197 yds) in 402 Wheat or 128 Cranberry

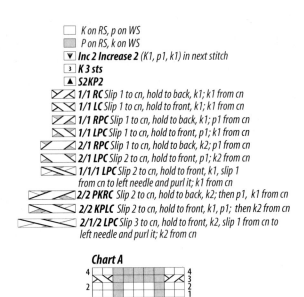

K on RS, p on WS

P on RS, k on WS

Inc 2 Increase 2 (K1, p1, k1) in next stitch

3 **K 3 sts**

▲ **S2KP2**

1/1 RC Slip 1 to cn, hold to back, k1; k1 from cn

1/1 LC Slip 1 to cn, hold to front, k1; k1 from cn

1/1 RPC Slip 1 to cn, hold to back, k1; p1 from cn

1/1 LPC Slip 1 to cn, hold to front, p1; k1 from cn

2/1 RPC Slip 1 to cn, hold to back, k2; p1 from cn

2/1 LPC Slip 2 to cn, hold to front, p1; k2 from cn

1/1/1 LPC Slip 2 to cn, hold to front, k1, slip 1
from cn to left needle and purl it; k1 from cn

2/2 PKRC Slip 2 to cn, hold to back, k2; then p1, k1 from cn

2/2 KPLC Slip 2 to cn, hold to front, k1, p1; then k2 from cn

2/1/2 LPC Slip 3 to cn, hold to front, k2, slip 1 from cn to
left needle and purl it; k2 from cn

Chart A

4
3
2
1

9 sts

Chart B

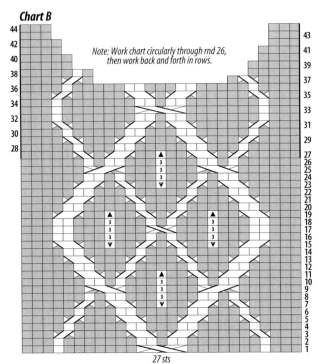

Note: Work chart circularly through rnd 26, then work back and forth in rows.

27 sts

HAT

Work doubled band

With crochet hook and smaller circular needle, chain cast on 96 (104, 112, 120, 128) stitches. Place marker (pm) and join, being careful not to twist stitches. Work 5 (5½, 5½, 6, 6)" in Twisted Rib. Fold cast-on edge up to inside and join hem by knitting 1 stitch from needle together with 1 MC stitch from cast-on edge, removing waste yarn as you go (see photos, next page).

Work body

Change to larger needle.

Increase round * P1, [k1, p1] 0 (1, 2, 3, 4) times, knit into front and back (kf&b) of next stitch, k3, p5, k2, p3, kf&b, p6, k1, kf&b, k2, p7, kf&b, p2, k2, p5,

k2, p1, kf&b, k1, [p1, k1] 0 (1, 2, 3, 4) times; repeat from * once more—106 (114, 122, 130, 138) stitches.

Begin Moss stitch and Charts A and B: Round 1 * Work 4 (6, 8, 10, 12) stitches in Moss stitch, 9 stitches Chart A, 27 stitches Chart B, 9 stitches Chart A, 4 (6, 8, 10, 12) stitches Moss stitch; repeat from * once more. Continue in patterns as established through round 26 of Chart B.

Divide work

Next row (RS) Continue patterns, work 55 (59, 63, 67, 71) stitches and place remaining stitches on hold—53 (57, 61, 65, 69) stitches on needle after S2KP2 has been worked. Work back and forth in rows on these stitches through row 36 of Chart B.

30

Shape neck

Next row (RS) Work 20 (22, 24, 26, 28) stitches, join 2nd ball of yarn and bind off 13 stitches, work to end. Working both sides at same time, bind off from each neck edge 2 stitches once, 1 stitch twice—16 (18, 20, 22, 24) stitches each side. Work 1 row even. Place stitches on hold.

Work remaining half of hat in same way, beginning with Row 3 of Chart A and Row 27 of Chart B. Join shoulders, using 3-needle bind-off.

Neckband

With RS facing and smaller double-pointed needles (dpn), pick up and knit 54 stitches evenly around neck edge. Pm, join and work in rounds as follows:

Rounds 1–6 * P1, k1 tbl; repeat from *.
Round 7 * K2tog; repeat from *—27 stitches.
Round 8 * K1, k2tog; repeat from *—18 stitches.
Cut yarn. Run tail through remaining stitches, pull together tightly and secure to WS.

Sleeves

With RS facing and larger dpn, begin at underarm and pick up and knit 34 stitches evenly around armhole. Pm, join and work in rounds as follows:

Round 1 [P1, k1] 3 times, p1, 9 stitches Chart A, p2, 9 stitches Chart A, [k1, p1] 3 times, k1.
Continue in patterns, working 7 stitches at beginning and end of round in Moss stitch, AT SAME TIME, decrease 1 stitch at beginning and end of round every 6th round 6 times—22 stitches. Work even until sleeve measures 5½" from beginning. Change to smaller dpn. Work 6 rounds in Twisted Rib. Bind off in rib pattern. Block hat.

Step-by-step hemming

1 Ribbed piece with contrasting chain cast-on is ready to work fold-up hem.

2 Fold ribbing in half to inside so that cast-on row is even with stitches on the needle.

3 Insert right needle purlwise into first main-color cast-on stitch.

4 Pull gently on contrasting yarn to "pop" it out of stitch that is still on right needle. If the yarn doesn't come out easily, you may have picked up from the wrong end of the chain. If so, try the alternate method (6).

5 Place cast-on stitch onto left needle and knit 2 together with next stitch on needle. Continue in this way around the entire piece.

6 Alternate method: remove waste yarn by "unzipping" the cast-on and placing all the cast-on stitches onto a spare needle. Fold cast-on row to inside as in Step 2. Knit 2 together working 1 stitch from each needle as shown.

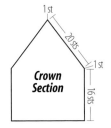

Tradition has a strong place in knitting, but using updated construction techniques to create a timeless piece is more in keeping with the best of the modern knitter. This project will satisfy both urges. The result is a special headpiece that will 'wow' all your friends.

Designed by Maureen Mason-Jamieson

Four Corners

INTERMEDIATE +

One size
Circumference 22"

10cm/4"

44

22

• over garter stitch (knit every row)

1 2 **3** 4 5 6

• Light weight
A & B • 125 yds
C • 75 yds

• 4mm/US6 , or size to obtain gauge,
40cm/16" long

• two 4mm/US6

• 3.75mm/F

&

• stitch marker
• tapestry needle

32

Notes

1 See *Techniques,* page 76, for SK2P, garter stitch graft, knit cast-on and tassels. **2** Use knit cast-on throughout.

Basic Crown Shaping

(**Note** Work crown sections in 2-row stripes with A and B; switch color every RS row.)

Row 1 and all WS rows Knit with color of previous row.
Row 2 (RS) K15, [SK2P, k18] twice, SK2P, k15.
Row 4 K33, SK2P, k33.
Row 6 K14, [SK2P, k15] twice, SK2P, k14.
Row 8 K29, SK2P, k29.
Row 10 K13, [SK2P, k12] twice, SK2P, k13.
Row 12 K25, SK2P, k25.
Row 14 K12, [SK2P, k9] twice, SK2P, k12.
Row 16 K21, SK2P, k21.
Row 18 K11, [SK2P, k6] twice, SK2P, k11.
Row 20 K17, SK2P, k17.
Row 22 K10, [SK2P, k3] twice, SK2P, k10.
Row 24 K13, SK2P, k13.
Row 26 K9, [SK2P] 3 times, k9.
Row 28 K9, slip 1, k1, psso, k10—20 stitches.

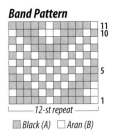

Band Pattern

11
10

5

1

— 12-st repeat —

☐ Black (A) ☐ Aran (B)

Crown Section

1st

20 sts

1st

16 sts

HAT
Crown Section 1

With A, cast on 75 stitches. Work 28 rows of Basic Crown Shaping. Cut yarn, leaving a 15" tail of A for grafting. Divide stitches evenly between 2 double-pointed needles (10/10). Graft stitches, using garter stitch graft.

Crown Section 2

With RS facing and B, pick up and knit 38 stitches along right edge of crown section just worked as follows (see diagram above): 16 stitches from lower edge to corner, 1 stitch in corner, 20 stitches to top point and 1 stitch in point, then cast on 37 stitches—75 stitches. Work 28 rows of Basic Crown Shaping. Graft stitches with B.

PATONS Astra (acrylic; 50g; 178 yds) in Black (A), Aran (B), and Cardinal (C)

Crown Section 3

Work as for Crown Section 2, except reverse colors.

Crown Section 4

With RS facing and B, pick up and knit 38 stitches along Crown Section 3, then join first and last crown sections as follows: Pick up and knit 20 stitches along left edge of Crown Section 1 from point to corner, 1 stitch in corner, and 16 stitches from corner to lower edge—75 stitches. Work 28 rows of Basic Crown Shaping. Graft stitches with B.

Band

Turn hat inside out and with WS facing and C, pick up and knit 29 stitches along lower edge of each section—116 stitches. Place marker and join. Knit 16 rounds. Purl 1 round (turning ridge). Cut yarn. With A, knit 1 round.
Next round [K3, knit into front and back of next stitch] 28 times, k4—144 stitches.
Begin Band Pattern: Round 1 [Work 12-stitch repeat of chart on page 32] 12 times. Work through Round 11. Cut B. With A, knit 1 round.
Next round [K3, k2tog] 28 times, k4—116 stitches. Cut A. With C, knit 1 round, purl 1 round. Bind off. Cut C, leaving a 1-yard tail.

Finishing

Fold band to RS at turning ridge and sew bound-off edge neatly to body, covering pick-up edge.
With C, make a 3" tassel. With 2 strands of A, leaving a 3" tail to start, crochet a 3" chain. Fasten off, leaving a 3" tail. Thread chain through center of tassel knob. Draw tails through center top point of hat, forming a loop, and secure to WS.

13

A simple hat and scarf set is given elegance with the addition of beads. Pre-stringing the beads is essential for fun and easy knitting—the beads simply slide between stitches as you knit.

Designed by Jane Davis

Beaded Ascot & Cloche

INTERMEDIATE

One size
ASCOT 6½" x 40"
CLOCHE circumference 21"

10cm/4"

24

17

• over stockinette stitch
(knit on RS, purl on WS)

1 2 3 **4** 5 6

• Medium weight
ASCOT • 215 yds
CLOCHE • 130 yds

• 5mm/US8, or size to obtain gauge

&

• beads that fit onto yarn (size 5 or 6),
CLOCHE 693 (48g or 2¼ oz)
ASCOT 506 (35g or 1½ oz)
• 8" length of sewing thread, beading
needle, stitch holder & yarn needle

Notes

1 See *Techniques*, page 76, for loop cast-on and grafting. *2* Use loop cast-on throughout, casting on tightly.

CLOCHE

String 693 beads onto one skein of yarn. Slide 126 beads into position, ready to work cast-on row.

Begin Beading Chart for Cloche: Cast-on row Cast on 3 stitches, [slide 6 beads to needle, cast on 4 stitches] 20 times, slide 6 beads to needle, cast on 3 stitches—86 stitches, 126 beads.

Row 1 (RS) Slide 105 beads into position, k2, * p1, slide 5 beads to needle, p1, k2; repeat from *. Work as established through chart Row 11. Continue in k2, p2 rib as established (without beads) until piece measures 8½" from beginning; end with a RS row. (From now on, this side will be referred to as the WS.)

Shape crown

Row 1 (RS) [K2tog, k2] 21 times, k2tog—64 stitches.

Row 2 and all WS rows Purl.

Row 3 [K2, k2tog] 16 times—48 stitches.

Row 5 [K2, k2tog] 12 times—36 stitches.

Row 7 [K2, k2tog] 9 times—27 stitches.

Row 9 [K2, k2tog] 6 times, k3—21 stitches.

Row 11 [K2, k2tog] 5 times, k1—16 stitches.

Row 12 Purl.

Cut yarn, leaving a 24" tail. Run tail through remaining stitches and pull together tightly, then sew seam (reversing seam at last 2" for fold-back cuff). Cut a 36" length of yarn, fold up cuff, and whip stitch in place with length of yarn, working on WS of cuff.

ASCOT

First half

String 253 beads onto one skein of yarn. Slide 42 beads into position, ready to work cast-on row.

Begin Beading Chart for Ascot: Cast-on row

Cast on 3 stitches, [slide 6 beads to needle, cast on 4 stitches] 6 times, slide 6 beads to needle, cast on 3 stitches—30 stitches, 42 beads.

Row 1 (RS) Slide 35 beads into position, k2, * p1, slide 5 beads to needle, p1, k2; repeat from *. Work as established through chart Row 24, then repeat Rows 23 and 24 until piece measures 20" from beginning; end with a WS row. Place stitches on hold.

Second half

Work as for first half. Graft live stitches of 2 halves together.

Finishing

Block piece.

36

Beading Chart for Ascot

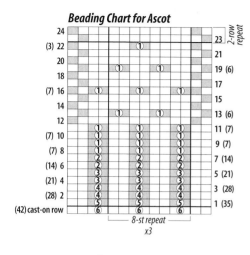

24
(3) 22
20
18
(7) 16
14
12
(7) 10
(7) 8
(14) 6
(21) 4
(28) 2
(42) cast-on row

23
21
19 (6)
17
15
13 (6)
11 (7)
9 (7)
7 (14)
5 (21)
3 (28)
1 (35)

2-row repeat

8-st repeat
x3

Beading Chart for Cloche

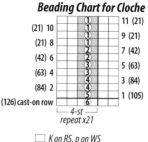

(21) 10
(21) 8
(42) 6
(63) 4
(84) 2
(126) cast-on row

11 (21)
9 (21)
7 (42)
5 (63)
3 (84)
1 (105)

4-st
repeat x21

☐ K on RS, p on WS
▨ P on RS, k on WS
▨(#) On RS: P1, slide number
of beads indicated, p1.
On WS: K1, slide number
of beads indicated, k1.
(#) Number of beads in row

*MISSION FALLS 1824 Wool (wool; 50g; 85 yds)
in Amethyst*

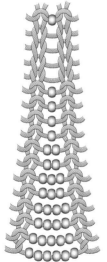

**Place beads between
2 purl stitches**

Beading Tips (see illustration at left)
Here are tips for knitting with beads:

1 To get the beads onto the yarn, tie an 8" piece of thread tightly around the yarn, near the tail, then thread it with a long beading needle and string your beads.

2 It's easier to count beads 5 at a time, sliding 2, then 3, and saying "five, ten, fifteen" and so on. I always count my beads twice, once as I string them, then once again after they are all on the yarn.

3 Be sure to pull your stitches tightly on either side of a bead section when you are sliding 3 or more beads between stitches. This way you won't have gaps of yarn hanging loosely between beads and stitches.

4 To make your knitting easier and more portable, place yarn in a basket or bowl.

Then slide the beads as you need them, letting the yarn pile loosely into the container. Otherwise, you will have to constantly wind and unwind the beaded section of the yarn when you need to move beads up or down the skein.

5 Before beginning each row, slide the number of beads you require for that row (the number in parentheses on the charts) up the yarn, so they are about four or five inches from the needle. Move about 2–3" of beads between your hand and the needle, so you can easily slide them into place as you knit.

6 In my cold-weather designs I always place beads where they won't touch the skin, since cold glass beads defeat the purpose of a scarf or hat.

For head-to-hand warmth, knit up this romantic set. The practical, classic 100% wool yarn provides the quality that will keep this set going for years to come. It is easy to make these pieces smaller or larger by decreasing or increasing the number of stitches in the seed stitch sections.

Designed by Penny Ollman

Snowbound Aran

EASY +

One size
HAT circumference 21"
COWL height 11½"
GLOVES circumference 8" x length 8½"

10cm/4"

35
18

• over seed stitch

1 2 3 **4** 5 6

• Medium weight
HAT • 225 yds
COWL • 225 yds
GLOVES • 180 yds

• 4.5mm/US7, or size to obtain gauge,
40cm/16" and 60cm/24" long

&

• stitch marker
• cable needle (cn)

Notes

1 See *Techniques,* page 76, for pompons.
2 Cowl and hat are worked circularly; gloves are worked back and forth in rows.

Seed stitch

Row 1 * P1, k1; repeat from *. **Row 2** Knit the purl stitches and purl the knit stitches. Repeat Row 2 for seed stitch.

HAT

With 16" needle, cast on 114 stitches. Place marker and join, being careful not to twist stitches.
Begin k2, p1 rib: Round 1 * K2, p1; repeat from *. Repeat Round 1 until piece measures 1".
Begin chart pattern and seed stitch: Round 1
[Work 35 stitches of chart pattern, 22

Chart Pattern

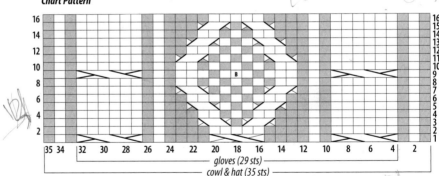

gloves (29 sts)
cowl & hat (35 sts)

☐ K on RS, p on WS
▨ P on RS, k on WS
B **MB Make Bobble** *[(K1, p1) twice, k1] in next stitch, turn; p5, turn; k5, turn; p5, turn; k5tog*
2/1 RC *Slip (sl) 1 to cn, hold to back, k2; k1 from cn*
2/1 LC *Sl 2 to cn, hold to front, k1; k2 from cn*
2/1 RPC *Sl 1 to cn, hold to back, k2; p1 from cn*
2/1 LPC *Sl 2 to cn, hold to front, p1; k2 from cn*
2/1/2 LPC *Sl 3 to cn, hold to front, k2; sl 1 st from cn to left needle and purl it; k2 from cn*
3/3 LC *Sl1 3 to cn, hold to front, k3; k3 from cn*

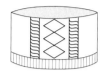

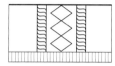

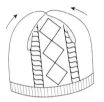

PATONS Classic Wool (wool; 100g; 223 yd) in 202 Aran

stitches in seed stitch] twice. Continue in patterns as established until 16 rounds of chart have been worked 3 times, then work round 1 once more. Bind off.

Finishing
Fold hat so that 35 chart stitches meet at center, with seed stitch at sides. Sew seam at top of hat. Fold top corners up to meet at center and sew in place. Make 3" pompon and attach to top of hat.

COWL
With 24" needle, cast on 138 stitches. Place marker and join, being careful not to twist stitches. **Begin k2, p1 rib: Round 1** * K2, p1; repeat from *. Repeat Round 1 until piece measures 1". **Begin chart pattern and seed stitch: Round 1** [Work 35 stitches of chart pattern, 11 stitches in seed stitch] 3 times. Continue in patterns as established until 16 rounds of chart have been worked 5 times, then work Round 1 once more. Work 1" in k2, p1 rib. Bind off.

GAUNTLET GLOVES
Left Glove
With 16" needle, cast on 50 stitches. Do not join. **Begin k2, p1 rib: Row 1** (RS) K1, p1, * k2, p1; repeat from *, end knit 3. **Row 2** P3, * k1, p2; repeat from *, end last repeat p1. Repeat Rows 1 and 2 until piece measures 1", end with a WS row.

Begin chart pattern: Row 1 (RS) K1, p1, work chart stitches 4-32 (over 29 stitches), [p1, k1] 9 times, k1. Continue in patterns as established, working stitches outside chart in rib pattern, until 16 rows of chart have been worked twice, then work Rows 1-5 once more.
Divide for thumb opening
Next row (WS) Continue in patterns, work 45 stitches, join 2nd ball of yarn and work to end. Working both sides at same time, continue patterns (omitting 3/3 LC at thumb opening) through chart Row 16, then work Row 1 once more. Using 1 ball of yarn for all stitches, work 1" in k2, p1 rib (begin with Row 2). Bind off.

Finishing
Sew side seam.

Right Glove
Work to correspond to left glove, reversing patterns and thumb opening placement. **Begin k2, p1 rib: Row 1** (RS) K1, * k2, p1; repeat from *, end k1. **Row 2** P1, * k1, p2; repeat from *, end last repeat p3. **Begin chart pattern: Row 1** (RS) K1, [k1, p1] 9 times, work chart stitches 4-32 (over 29 stitches), p1, k1.
Divide for thumb opening
Next row (WS) Continue in patterns, work 5 stitches, join 2nd ball of yarn and work to end.

15

INTERMEDIATE

TAM
One size
Circumference 24"

10cm/4"

28
24

• over Pattern A

1 2 **3** 4 5 6

• Light weight
MC • 175 yds
CC • 150 yds

• 3.75mm/US5, or size to obtain gauge,
40cm/16" long

• four 3.75mm/US5

&

• stitch marker
• 10½" dinner plate (or circle of cardboard)
for blocking

This set uses moving stripes to create a barber-pole effect. Moving the marker at the beginning of alternate rounds prevents a jog in the pattern. The mitten tops are shaped so that either mitten can be worn on either hand, allowing you to wear the stripes curling 'in' one day and curling 'out' the next. The ribbing on the tam is reversed after the turning round so that it will 'nest' nicely.

Designed by Lois Young

Barber Pole

Notes
1 See *Techniques,* page 76, for knit into front and back (kf&b), SSK, and S2KP2. **2** Change to double pointed needles (dpns) when needed. **3** Knit all stitches, unless indicated otherwise. **4** When pieces are complete, fasten off stitches as follows: Cut yarn, leaving a 6" tail. Pull tail through remaining stitches tightly and secure to WS.

Move Marker
Remove marker, slip (sl) 1 stitch (MM1) or 2 stitches (MM2) purlwise with yarn in back, replace marker.
(**Note** To avoid a long strand of yarn from carry after marker has been moved 2 stitches, work to last 3 stitches of round, insert right needle knitwise into next stitch and under strand, knit stitch and strand together, knit last 2 stitches of round. See page 85.)

Pattern A (6-stitch repeat)
Knit every round as follows:
Rounds 1 and 2 * 3CC, 3MC; repeat from *.
Round 3 MM2, * 3MC, 3CC; repeat from *.
Round 4 * 3MC, 3CC; repeat from *.
Round 5 MM2, * 3CC, 3MC; repeat from *.

Round 6 * 3CC, 3MC; repeat from *.
Repeat Rounds 3-6 for Pattern A.

Pattern B (6-stitch repeat)
Knit every round as follows:
Rounds 1 and 2 * 3CC, 3MC; repeat from *.
Round 3 MM1, * 3CC, 3MC; repeat from *.
Round 4 * 3CC, 3MC; repeat from *.
Repeat Rounds 3 and 4 for Pattern B.

TAM
With circular needle and MC, cast on 96 stitches. Place marker (pm) and join, being careful not to twist stitches.
Rounds 1–8 * P1, k1; repeat from *.
Round 9 Purl (turning ridge).
Rounds 10–16 * K1, p1; repeat from *.
Round 17 * Knit in front and back (kf&b) of next stitch, p1; repeat from *—144 stitches. Work 36 rounds of Pattern A, ending with Round 4.

Shape crown
Round 1 MM2, * 3CC, 3MC; repeat from *.
Round 2 * [3CC, 3MC] twice, 3CC, k3tog with MC; repeat from *—128 stitches.
Round 3 MM2, * [3MC, 3CC] twice, 1MC, 3CC; repeat from *.
Round 4 * 3MC, 3CC, 3MC, 2CC, S2KP2 with MC, 2CC; repeat from *—112 stitches.

Round 5 MM2, * 3CC, 3MC, 5CC, 3MC; repeat from *.

Round 6 * 3CC, 3MC, 1CC, k3tog with CC, 1CC, 3MC; repeat from *—96 stitches.

Round 7 MM2, * 3MC, 3CC; repeat from *.

Round 8 * K3tog with MC, 3CC, 3MC, 3CC; repeat from *—80 stitches.

Round 9 MM2, * 1CC, 3MC, 3CC, 1MC, 2CC; repeat from *.

Round 10 * 1CC, 3MC, 2CC, S2KP2 with MC, 1CC; repeat from *—64 stitches.

Round 11 MM2, * 1MC, 5CC, 2MC; repeat from *.

Round 12 * 1MC, 1CC, k3tog with CC, 1CC, 2MC; repeat from *—48 stitches.

Round 13 MM2, * 1CC, 3MC, 2CC; repeat from *.

Round 14 * 1CC, k3tog with MC, 2CC; repeat from *—32 stitches.

Round 15 MM2, * 2CC, 1MC, 1CC; repeat from *.

Round 16 * 1CC, S2KP2 with MC; repeat from *—16 stitches.
Cut CC.

Round 17 * K2tog with MC; repeat from *—8 stitches. Fasten off.

Finishing

With MC, make one 1½" pompon and attach to top of tam. Dampen tam and place over dinner plate or cardboard circle. Let dry. Fold band to WS at turning ridge and sew in place.

DALE OF NORWAY Falk (superwash wool; 50g; 116 yds) 083 Charcoal (MC) and 4137 Brick Red (CC)

INTERMEDIATE
MITTENS
One size
Circumference 8"

10cm/4"

28
24
• over Pattern A

1 2 **3** 4 5 6
• Light weight
MC • 100 yds
CC • 80 yds

• 3.75mm/US5, or size to obtain gauge,
40cm/16" long

• four 3.75mm/US5

• stitch marker

MITTEN A

With dpns and MC, cast on 48 stitches. Pm and join, being careful not to twist stitches.

Rounds 1–24 * K1, p1; repeat from *. Work 19 rounds of Pattern A (page 42), ending with Round 3.

Mark thumb

Next round With contrasting waste yarn, knit 8, then return these 8 stitches to left needle, work Round 4 of Pattern A over all stitches. Work as established until 53 rounds of pattern have been worked from beginning, ending with Round 5.

Shape top

Round 1 * SSK with CC, 1CC, 3MC; repeat from *—40 stitches. **Round 2** MM2, * 2MC, 2CC, 1MC; repeat from *. **Round 3** * SSK with MC, 2CC, 1MC; repeat from *—32 stitches. **Round 4** MM2, * 2MC, 2CC; repeat from *. **Round 5** * 2MC, SSK with CC; repeat from *—24 stitches. **Round 6** MM2, * 2MC, 1CC; repeat from *. **Round 7** * SSK with MC, 1CC; repeat from *—16 stitches. **Round 8** MM1, * 1MC, 1CC; repeat from *. Cut CC. **Round 9** * SSK with MC; repeat from *—8 stitches. Fasten off.

Thumb

Carefully remove waste yarn, placing 8 loops from bottom and 8 from top on separate dpns. Place round marker at right end of lower dpn, then divide 16 stitches over 3 dpns.

Round 1 3MC, 3CC, 2MC, pick up and k1 stitch with MC, 3CC, 3MC, 2CC, pick up and k1 stitch with CC—18 stitches. Begin with Round 5, work 16 rounds of Pattern A, ending with Round 4.

Shape tip

Round 1 MM2, * k2tog with CC, 1CC, 3MC; repeat from *. **Round 2** * 2CC, 3MC; repeat from *. **Round 3** MM1, * k2tog with MC, 1MC, 2CC; repeat from *.
Round 4 * 2MC, 2CC; repeat from *. Cut CC.
Round 5 * K2tog with MC; repeat from *— 6 stitches. Fasten off.

MITTEN B

Work as for Mitten A to "shape top", except work Pattern B (page 42), and end with pattern Round 4.

Shape top

Round 1 MM1, * SSK with CC, 1CC, 3MC; repeat from *. **Round 2** * 2CC, 3MC; repeat from *. **Round 3** MM1, * 2CC, SSK with MC, 1MC; repeat from *. **Round 4** * 2CC, 2MC; repeat from *. **Round 5** MM1, * SSK with CC, 2MC; repeat from *.
Round 6 * 1CC, 2MC; repeat from *.
Round 7 MM1, * 1CC, SSK with MC; repeat from *. **Round 8** * 1CC, 1MC; repeat from *. Cut CC. **Round 9** * SSK with MC; repeat from *—8 stitches. Fasten off.

Thumb

Divide stitches as for Mitten A.
Round 1 3CC, 3MC, 2CC, pick up and k1 stitch with CC, 3MC, 3CC, 2MC, pick up and k1 stitch with MC—18 stitches. Begin with Round 3, work 16 rounds of Pattern B, ending with Round 4.

Shape tip

Rounds 1–4 Work as for Rounds 1–4 of "shape top". Cut CC. **Round 5** * SSK with MC; repeat from *—6 stitches. Fasten off.

Anna uses partial practice toes that are worked from the bottom up to create two novel hats. Once you get started, you'll want to make one for every member of the family.

Designed by Anna Zilboorg

Toe Hats

INTERMEDIATE

Child (Adult)
Circumference 18½ (20)"

10cm/4"

30 | 24

• over stockinette stitch (knit every round)

1 2 4 5 6

• Light weight
CHILD A • 75 yds
B • 60 yds
ADULT A • 100 yds
B & C • 50 yds each

• 3.25mm/US3, or size to obtain gauge,
40cm/16" long

• five 3.25mm/US3

&

• stitch marker

Notes

1 See *Techniques,* page 76, for SSK, S2KP2, invisible cast-on, loop cast-on (right & left), and grafting open stitches to cast-on edge.
2 Work toes first, then continue with rest of hat. **3** Change to double pointed needles when necessary.

Toes, make 7 (6)

With double-pointed needle (dpn) and A, cast on 4 stitches, using invisible cast-on. [Purl 1 row, knit 1 row] 2 (3) times. Place 4 cast-on stitches on 2nd dpn, removing waste yarn. (You now have a rectangle with 4 stitches at either end.) Return to working yarn and with RS facing and a 3rd dpn, pick up and knit 3 (5) stitches along side of rectangle; with a 4th dpn, knit 4 cast-on stitches; with free dpn, pick up and knit 3 (5) stitches along remaining edge of rectangle—2 dpns with 4 stitches each, 2 with 3 (5) stitches each. Knit 1 round. Rearrange stitches on dpns by moving first and last stitches from dpns that have 4 stitches on them to adjacent dpns—2 dpns with 2 stitches each, 2 with 5 (7) stitches each.
Increase round K2 from first dpn; right loop cast-on 1 stitch, knit to end of 2nd dpn, left loop cast-on 1 stitch; k2 from 3rd dpn; right loop cast-on 1 stitch, knit to end of 4th dpn, left loop cast-on 1 stitch—2 dpns with 2 stitches each, 2 with 7 (9) stitches each.
Next round Knit. Repeat last 2 rounds 5 times more—2 dpns with 2 stitches each, 2 with 17 (19) stitches each. Using last dpn worked (4th dpn), knit 1 from first dpn, slip (sl) remaining stitch on first dpn to 2nd dpn, sl first stitch on 3rd dpn onto 2nd dpn, sl remaining stitch on 3rd dpn onto 4th dpn—2 dpns with 19 (21) stitches each. With circular needle, * knit 1 stitch from front needle together with 1 stitch from back needle; repeat from * across. Cut yarn. Make 6 (5) more toes. For child's hat, do not cut yarn after last toe. When completed, toes will be lined up on the circular needle ready to proceed with the hat.

CHILD'S HAT

Crown

Place marker (pm), join and knit 1 round—133 stitches.
Next round K18, [k2tog, k17] 6 times, k2tog, removing marker and replacing it after k2tog—126 stitches. * With B, knit 2 rounds.

NATURALLY *Luxury DK (wool, mohair; 50g; 114 yds) Child: 909 Navy (A), and 993 Green (B)*

Decrease round Remove marker, sl 1, pm, [k15, S2KP2] 7 times—112 stitches. With A, knit 2 rounds.

Decrease round Remove marker, sl 1, pm, [k13, S2KP2] 7 times—98 stitches. Repeat from * 3 times more, working 2 fewer knit stitches before S2KP2 each decrease round—14 stitches. With B, knit 2 rounds.

Next round [K2tog] 7 times. Cut yarn. Draw tail through remaining stitches twice, and secure to WS.

Band

With WS of crown facing, circular needle and B, pick up and k19 stitches in purl bumps along base of each toe—133 stitches. Pm, join and knit 2 rounds.

Decrease round Remove marker, sl 1, pm, [k16, S2KP2] 7 times—119 stitches. Knit 2 rounds.

Next round With A, k2tog, * k1B, k1A; repeat from *, end k1B—118 stitches. Knit 12 rounds more, matching colors. Cut A. With B, knit 2 rounds.

I-cord bind-off

Cast on 3 stitches onto right needle, using loop cast-on, then sl them to left needle. * K2, SSK, sl 3 stitches from right to left needle; repeat from * until all stitches have been worked from left needle. Graft remaining 3 stitches to cast-on edge.

ADULT'S HAT

Make Bobble (MB) [(K1, yo) twice, k1] in next stitch, turn; sl 1 purlwise with yarn in front (wyif), k4, turn; sl 1 purlwise with yarn in back (wyib), p4, turn; sl 1 wyif, k4, turn. Pass 2nd, 3rd, 4th and 5th stitches, one at a time, over first stitch, then k1 (bobble complete).

Crown

Pm, join and knit 2 rounds with C, 1 round with B—126 stitches.

Begin Chart A: Round 1 Work 7-stitch repeat of chart 18 times. Work through Round 18. Knit 1 round with B, 2 rounds with C.

Next round [P19, p2tog] 6 times—120 stitches.

Bobble round * MB with C, k3 with B; repeat from *.

Begin Chart B: Round 1 Work 12-stitch repeat of chart 10 times. Work through chart Round 27. Cut yarn. Draw tail through remaining 10 stitches twice and secure to WS.

Band

With WS facing, circular needle and B, pick up and knit 20 stitches in purl bumps along base of each toe—120 stitches. Pm, join and work 5 rounds in k1, p1 rib. Bind off in rib.

Color key
■ Fuchsia (A)
■ Navy (B)
■ Bronze (C)

Chart A

Chart B

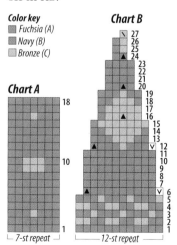

└ 7-st repeat ┘   └ 12-st repeat ┘

Stitch key ▲ S2KP2 ◥ SSK

▽ *At beginning of round only, remove marker, slip 1 purlwise with yarn in back, replace round marker (marker moved 1 st to left).*

NATURALLY *Luxury DK (wool, mohair; 50g; 114 yds) Adult: 933 Fuchsia (A), 909 Navy (B), and 994 Bronze (C)*

17

In Knitting Around, Elizabeth Zimmermann espouses 'the two great rules of Fair Isle knitting: never carry more than two colors on a given round and avoid a carry greater than five stitches long.' Fair Isle knitting exemplifies that nearly perfect combination, maximum design with minimal effort. Knit a few gift sets, and have fun creating new color combinations!

Designed by Michele Woodford

Fair Isle Friends

INTERMEDIATE
HATS
Child 4/6 (8/10; Adult, M, L)
18" (19 ½; 20, 22 ½)"

MITTENS
XS/S (M, L)

10cm/4"

24

16
• over stockinette stitch (knit all rounds)
and chart pattern using larger needles

1 2 3 **4** 5 6

• Medium weight
HAT AND MITTENS
MC • 100 (150, 175, 200) yds
• small amounts of CC colors

• two 4.5mm/US7 and two 5mm/US8, or
size to obtain gauge

• stitch markers and small stitch holder

RED CAP

With smaller double-pointed needles (dpn) and MC, cast on 72 (78, 84, 90) stitches and divide evenly over 3 dpns. Place marker (pm) and join, being careful not to twist stitches. Knit 8 (8, 8, 12) rounds. Change to larger dpn. Knit 4 rounds more with MC. Work 33 rounds of Chart A, then continue with MC only, AT SAME TIME, after 24 rounds of chart have been worked, begin decreases:
Round 25 * K5 (5, 7, 8), k2tog; repeat from *, end k2 (1, 3, 0)—62 (67, 75, 81) stitches. Work 1 round even.
Round 27 * K4 (4, 6, 7), k2tog; repeat from *, end k2 (1, 3, 0)—52 (56, 66, 72) stitches. Work 1 round even. Continue to decrease every other round (working 1 stitch less between decreases each time) until 12 (12, 12, 9) stitches remain. Cut yarn, draw through stitches tightly and fasten off.

Finishing

Top loop

With smaller dpn and MC, cast on 3 stitches. Work 6 rows in stockinette stitch (St st) (knit all rows), increase 1 stitch each side on 3rd row—5 stitches. Work 6 rows of Chart B. With MC, work 6 rows in St st, decrease 1 stitch each side on 3rd row—3 stitches. Bind off. Fold loop in half and sew to top of cap.

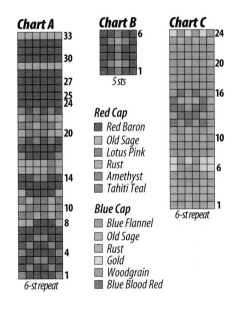

Chart A
33
30
27
25
24

20

14

10
8

4

1
6-st repeat

Chart B
6

1
5 sts

Red Cap
■ Red Baron
□ Old Sage
■ Lotus Pink
■ Rust
■ Amethyst
■ Tahiti Teal

Blue Cap
■ Blue Flannel
□ Old Sage
■ Rust
■ Gold
■ Woodgrain
■ Blue Blood Red

Chart C
24

20

16

10

6

1
6-st repeat

BROWN SHEEP *Lamb's Pride Worsted (wool, mohair; 113g; 190 yds)* **Red colorway** *M-81 Red Baron (MC), M-47 Tahiti Teal, M-38 Lotus Pink, M-69 Old Sage, M-97 Rust, and M-62 Amethyst*

Blue colorway *M-82 Blue Flannel (MC), M-69 Old Sage, M-97 Rust, M-14 Gold, M-98 Woodgrain, and M-80 Blue Blood Red*

BLUE CAP

With smaller dpn and MC, cast on and work as for red cap, working 24 rounds of Chart C instead of Chart A. Knit with MC to end, AT SAME TIME, follow decreases as given for red cap—12 (12, 12, 9) stitches remain. Cut yarn, draw through stitches tightly and fasten off.

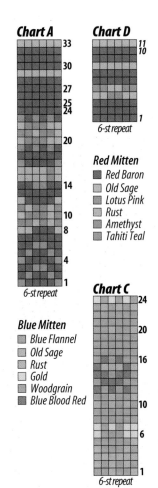

Chart A

33
30
27
25
24
20
14
10
8
4
1

6-st repeat

Blue Mitten
- Blue Flannel
- Old Sage
- Rust
- Gold
- Woodgrain
- Blue Blood Red

Chart D

11
10

1

6-st repeat

Red Mitten
- Red Baron
- Old Sage
- Lotus Pink
- Rust
- Amethyst
- Tahiti Teal

Chart C

24
20
16
10
6
1

6-st repeat

RED MITTENS
Right
With smaller dpn and MC, cast on 28 (32, 36) stitches and divide evenly over 3 dpns. Place marker (pm), and join being careful not to twist stitches. Knit 9 (14, 14) rounds, increase 2 (4, 6) stitches on last round—30 (36, 42) stitches. Change to larger dpn. Knit 5 (4, 4) rounds more with MC. Work Rounds 14-23 (8-23, 8-23) of Chart A.

Thumb opening

(**Note** Work thumb opening as follows: on first round, place 5 (6, 7) stitches on hold, join 2nd ball of yarn and knit to end; on next round, cast on 5 (6, 7) stitches over stitches on hold.) Work thumb opening on first round and knit 0 (2, 4) rounds MC, then work rounds 1-11 of Chart D. With MC, knit 1 (3, 3) rounds.

Shape top

Work with MC as follows:

Next round * K2tog, k13 (16, 19)*, pm, repeat between *'s once. Continue to decrease 1 stitch after each marker every other round 5 (8, 11) times more—18 stitches. Cut yarn, draw through stitches tightly and fasten off.

Thumb

With larger dpn and MC, k5 (6, 7) stitches from holder, then pick up and k5 (6, 7) stitches along cast-on edge—10 (12, 14) stitches. Divide stitches evenly on 3 dpns. Pm, join and knit 8 (10, 12)

rounds. Change to Rust. Knit every round, decrease 1 stitch each side every other round 2 (3, 4) times—6 stitches. Cut yarn, draw through stitches tightly and fasten off.

Left
Work as for right mitten, working thumb opening at end of round, instead of at beginning of round.

BLUE MITTENS
Right
With smaller dpn and MC, cast on and work as for right red mitten until there are 30 (36, 42) stitches. Change to larger dpn. Knit 4 rounds more with MC. Work Rounds 6-16 (1-16, 1-16) of Chart C.

Thumb opening

With MC, knit 4 (6, 6) rounds, AT SAME TIME, work thumb opening on first round (see Note under thumb opening for right red mitten). Work Rounds 20-24 of Chart C. Knit 3 (5, 7) rounds MC.

Shape top, thumb

Follow instructions for right red mitten, changing to Old Sage instead of Rust.

Left
Work as for right mitten, working thumb opening at end of round, instead of at beginning of round.

18

Nordkapp, Norway at 71° 10' 21" (the north cape of Norway) is the farthest north point in Europe that you can visit. When you do, wear this cuffed cap with its 3-D polar bear tassels.

Designed by Sue Flanders

Nordkapp

INTERMEDIATE

HAT
Child's Medium
Circumference 17½"

10cm/4"

25
22
• over stockinette stitch
(knit all rounds), using larger needles

1 2 **3** 4 5 6

• Light weight
A • 150 yds
B • 110 yds

• 3.75mm/US5, or size to obtain gauge,
40cm/16" long

• four each size 3.25/US3 and 3.75mm/US5

&

• stitch markers and holders

Notes
1 See *Techniques,* page 76, for Make 1 (M1), loop cast-on, SSK, I-cord, and weaving the carries. **2** When carrying yarn over several stitches, weave the carried yarn along the WS of the work. **3** Change to double-pointed needles (dpns) when necessary.

HAT
Lining
With circular needle and B, cast on 96 stitches, place marker (pm) and join, being careful not to twist stitches. Knit 30 rounds. Purl 2 rounds (turning ridge).

Chart A

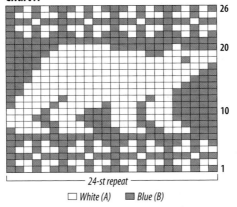

— 24-st repeat —

☐ White (A)   ■ Blue (B)

Knit 1 round.
Work 26 rounds of Chart A. With B, knit 1 round, purl 2 rounds. Cut B. With A, knit every round for 2¼", pm (a different color than round marker) after 24th, 48th and 72nd stitches on last round.

Top decreases
Next round * SSK, knit to 3 stitches before marker, k2tog, k1, slip marker (sm); repeat from *. Repeat this round until 12 stitches remain. Cut yarn, leaving a 6" tail. Run tail through remaining stitches and tighten.

Finishing
Turn lining to inside and sew along top edge of Chart A pattern. To block hat, steam lightly with damp cloth. A pressing ham works nicely inside the hat to maintain head shape.

Mini-polar bear tassels (make 3)
(**Note** The bears are worked from rump to nose.) With smaller dpns and A, cast on 20 stitches, divided over 3 dpns (8-4-8). Join, being careful not to twist stitches.

SWEDISH YARN IMPORTS Peer Gynt (wool; 50g; 100 yds) in colors 17 White (A) and 656 Blue (B)

INTERMEDIATE
MITTEN

Child's Medium
Circumference 7"
Length of hand 6"

10cm/4"

25
22
• over stockinette stitch
(knit all rounds), using larger needles

1 2 **3** 4 5 6

Light weight
A • 150 yds
B • 90 yds

• 3.25mm/US3 and 3.75mm/US5

&

•stitch markers

Round 1 Knit, pm after 10th stitch.
Rounds 2–5 Knit to 1 stitch before marker, loop cast on 1 stitch, k1, sm, k1, loop cast on 1 stitch, knit to end.
Round 6 Knit to 4 stitches before end of round, bind off 4 stitches (leg bind-off).
Round 7 Bind off another 4 stitches (leg bind-off), knit to end of round—20 stitches (4-12-4).
Round 8 Knit, pulling yarn tight to close gap of leg bind-off.
Rounds 9 and 11 Knit to 2 stitches before marker, k2tog, sm, SSK, knit to end.
Round 10 Knit.
Round 12 Knit to end, cast on 4 stitches.
Round 13 Cast on 4 stitches, knit to 2 stitches before marker, k2tog, sm, SSK, knit to end.
Rounds 14, 16 and 17 Knit.
Round 15 Repeat Round 9.
Round 18 Repeat Round 6.
Round 19 Repeat Round 7—12 stitches (4-4-4).
Round 20 Knit to end of 2nd needle, [turn, p4, turn, k4] twice (for neck), then pick up and knit 2 stitches along left edge of neck down to 3rd needle, knit to end.
Round 21 K4, pick up and knit 2 stitches along edge of neck up to 2nd needle, knit to end. Reposition the 16 stitches so that they are divided 7-2-7.
Round 22 Knit to 3 stitches before marker, k2tog, k1, sm, k1, SSK, knit to end.
Rounds 23–26 Repeat Round 22 four times—6 stitches.

Cut yarn, leaving a 6" tail. Run tail through remaining stitches and pull tight. Seam legs. Stuff with small amount of fiber fill. Seam rumps. If desired, make French knot eyes with B on each side of bear's head. Work a 3-stitch I-cord for 4" for each bear and attach to center back of bear. Attach I-cord to top of hat.

LEFT MITTEN
Gauntlet
With larger dpns and B, cast on 54 stitches, divided evenly over 3 dpns. Join, being careful not to twist stitches. Purl 1 round. Knit 1 round.
Work 17 rounds of Chart B. Cut A.
Next round With B, knit.
Next round * P2tog, p1; repeat from *— 36 stitches.
Next round Purl. Cut yarn and set aside.

Chart B

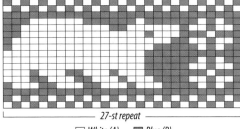

27-st repeat

□ White (A) ■ Blue (B)

Ribbing
With smaller dpns and A, cast on 36 stitches, divided evenly over 3 dpns. Join, being careful not to twist stitches.

Work in k1, p1 rib for 3".

Join gauntlet and rib

Slip (sl) rib down inside center of gauntlet. Hold 2 needles in left hand with the gauntlet needle in front and the ribbing needle in the back. Using a larger dpn in the right hand and A, * knit 1 stitch from front needle together with 1 stitch from back needle; repeat from * until both layers are joined.

Hand

Round 1 * K6, M1; repeat from *—42 stitches. Sl first 2 stitches of next round to right needle (for new start of round). Place marker after 38th and 41st stitches (for thumb gusset).

Round 2 Knit to first marker, sl marker (sm), M1, knit to 2nd marker, M1, sm, knit to end.

Rounds 3–5 Knit.

Rounds 6–17 Repeat Rounds 2–5 three times—11 stitches between markers.

Rounds 18–19 Knit.

Round 20 Knit to first marker, remove markers and place 11 stitches on hold (for thumb hole), cast on 3 stitches onto right needle, knit to end. Knit every round until hand measures 5".

Top decreases

Pm after 21st stitch.

Decrease round SSK, knit to 3 stitches before marker, k2tog, k1, sm, SSK,

knit to 3 stitches before marker, k2tog, k1. Repeat Decrease round until 6 stitches remain. Cut yarn, leaving a 6" tail. Run tail through remaining stitches and pull tight.

Thumb

Place 11 stitches from holder divided onto 2 dpns, then with 3rd needle, pick up and knit 5 stitches along thumb hole cast-on—16 stitches. Join A and knit 12 rounds.

Decrease round 1 [SSK, k4, k2tog] twice—12 stitches.

Round 2 [SSK, k2, k2tog] twice—8 stitches.

Round 3 [SSK, k2tog] twice—4 stitches. Cut yarn, run tail through stitches and pull tight.

RIGHT MITTEN

Work as for left mitten, except pm for thumb gusset after first and 4th stitches.

Finishing

Block mittens. When blocking gauntlet cuff, fold ribbing inside the palm of the mitten to avoid steaming the ribbing.

19

INTERMEDIATE

One size
Circumference 20½"

10cm/4"

34

28

• over color patterns

 2 3 4 5 6

• Super fine weight
W and B • 240 yds each

• 3.25mm/US3, or size to obtain gauge,
40cm/16" long

• six 3.25mm/US3

&

• stitch marker

Qiviut is the wonderfully warm, soft undercoat of the musk ox: a luxury fiber from the North countries. Ridges of purl divide these pattern bands. Big flakes graduate to smaller ones. Light zigs become dark zags. Fingertips, thumbs and hat crown shape over a small dot pattern. The yarn is so soft it melts, and the knitting is easy enough to enjoy.

Designed by Deborah Newton

Snowflakes

Notes

1 See *Techniques*, page 76, for Make 1 (M1), SSK and pompon. **2** When working with two colors, carry yarn not in use loosely across the WS, twisting as necessary to avoid long floats. Read all RS knit chart rows from right to left.

HAT

With circular needle and W, cast on 144 stitches. Place marker (pm) and join, being careful to not twist stitches. Purl 3 rounds. Work 25 rounds of Large Snowflake Pattern. With W, knit 1 round. Purl 3 rounds. Work 12 rounds of Zigzag Pattern, decrease 4 stitches evenly spaced on last round—140 stitches. Work Rounds 1-17 of Small Snowflake Pattern. With W, knit 1 round, decrease 20 stitches evenly—120 stitches. Purl 3 rounds. With B, knit 1 round, decrease 5 stitches evenly—115 stitches. Change to double pointed needles (dpn) as follows: ***Next round*** * with one dpn, work 21 stitches in Dot Pattern, begin and end where indicated, with W k2 (divider stitches); repeat from * 4 more times, using 4 more dpns, 23 stitches each. Keeping 2 stitch dividers in W, work in

pattern as established for 2 more rounds. Keeping in pattern, decrease 1 stitch before and after every divider on next round and every 3rd round 3 times, then every 2 rounds after until 3 stitches remain on each dpn (1B stitch, 2W stitches). Work 1 round even.
Next round With W, * k2tog, k1; repeat on each needle. Knit 1 round W, then slip yarn through remaining stitches. Make small pompom if desired and attach to top of hat.

Crown Chart

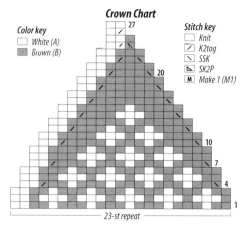

27

20

10

7

4

1

23-st repeat

Small Snowflake Chart

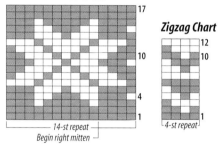

17

10

4

1

14-st repeat
Begin right mitten

Zigzag Chart

12

10

1

4-st repeat

Large Snowflake Chart

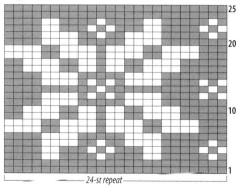

25

20

10

1

24-st repeat

DOWN NORTH'S 100% *Qiviut 2 ply fingering (25g; 140 yds) in Natural Brown (B) and
Bleached White (W)*

MITTEN

Mitten is one size, to fit average woman.
Measurements. Palm circumference: 8".

RIGHT MITTEN

Cuff

With W, cast on 76 stitches and divide among 3 needles. Place marker (pm) and join, taking care not to twist cast-on row. Purl 3 rounds. Begin Zigzag Pattern where indicated and work until 12 rounds are complete, decrease 4 stitches evenly on last round—72 stitches. Arrange 24 stitches each on 3 needles. Begin Large Snowflake Pattern where indicated and work until 25 rounds are complete. With W, knit 1 round, then purl 3 rounds.

Hand section

With B, knit 1 round, decrease 15 stitches evenly on last round (5 decreases per needle)—57 stitches. Cut yarn. Move beginning of round marker 1 stitch to left. Divide stitches on 4 dpn as follows: 15 stitches on first needle of round, 14 stitches each on other 3 needles. Needles 1 and 2 are palm stitches, Needles 3 and 4 are back of hand stitches.

Set up thumb gusset and patterns

Next Round K2W (keep these 2 gusset outline stitches in W until thumb gusset is complete), k1B (first stitch of thumb gusset chart), k2W (keep these 2 outline stitches in W until thumb gusset is complete), then work Round 1 of Zigzag Pattern to end of round. While working solid color B pattern rows on thumb gusset, it is necessary to carry W very loosely along WS for outline stitches.

Continue to work in Zigzag Pattern and thumb gusset pattern, increase every 3rd round as shown, keeping outline sections in W, until 2 full repeats of Zigzag Pattern are complete (24 pattern rows). Work Rows 1 and 2 of Small Snowflake Pattern—26 rounds of thumb gusset chart complete. Place 21 thumb stitches (includes 4 outline stitches) on hold—10 stitches remain on this needle. Cast on 5 stitches to make 15 stitches on thumb needle and continue Small Snowflake Pattern until complete, and at the same time on last row, decrease 1 stitch at beginning of 2nd and 4th needles—13 stitches remain on these 2 needles—54 stitches total.

Next Round * On first needle, k1W (side stitch), work in Dot Pattern over 13 stitches; on 2nd needle, work in Dot Pattern over 12 stitches, end k1W (side stitch); repeat from * over next 2 needles. Keeping in pattern as established, keep side stitches in W throughout, work in pattern until hand section above thumb gusset measures 3", or to desired length.

Form mitten tip

Next Round (decrease round) * SSK with W, work to 1 stitch before next side stitch, k2tog with W; repeat from *. Work 1 round even, 1 decrease round, 1 even round. Repeat decrease round until 6 stitches remain. Slip (sl) 3 stitches each from front and back to separate needles. Sl 1, k2tog, psso on each needle. Cut and thread end through last stitches.

Thumb

Sl 21 stitches to 2 dpn. Work in outline and Dot Patterns as established across stitches over 2 needles, then with B, pick up 7 stitches in palm cast-on stitches to beginning—28 stitches.

Next Round Continue in Dot Pattern over 21 stitches as established; then on 3rd needle, (k1B, k1W) 3 times, end k1B (to form a vertical stripe pattern); repeat this every round.

Continue in patterns as established, decrease 1 stitch in Dot Pattern section (after first 2 outline stitches and before last 2 outline stitches) every other round until 11 stitches remain on first 2 needles—18 stitches total. Work even until thumb is desired length (approximately 3–4 more rounds).

TIP
Decrease 1 stitch before and after outline stitches until 2 stitches remain. Cut and draw end through 2 stitches and tighten. Make a 4" length of I-cord and attach at cuff in loop.

LEFT MITTEN
Work same as right mitten, except reverse placement of thumb gusset, placing it at the end of round instead of at beginning of round.

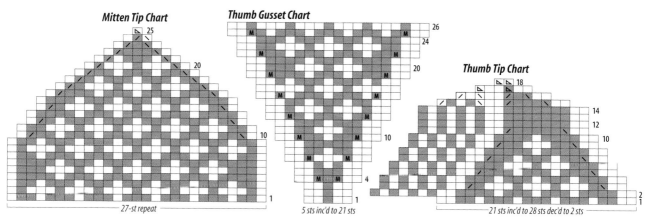

Mitten Tip Chart — 27-st repeat

Thumb Gusset Chart — 5 sts inc'd to 21 sts

Thumb Tip Chart — 21 sts inc'd to 28 sts dec'd to 2 sts

59

Roughly speaking, hats blocked on head-shaped bowls remain hats; those blocked on dinner plates become tams. Choose a design from the three given here and have fun with it. Vary the pattern and background colors, and the knitting will begin to take on a life of its own.

Designed by Mary Rowe

Kaleidoscopes & Tams

INTERMEDIATE +

One size
Circumference 22"

10cm/4"

32
28
• over stockinette stitch (knit all rounds), using larger needles

 2 3 4 5 6

Super fine weight
• 220 yds total of assorted colors

• 2.75mm/US2 and 3.25mm/US3, or size to obtain gauge, 40cm/16" long

•four 3.25mm/US3

&

• stitch marker

Notes
1 See *Techniques,* page 76, for chain cast-on, Make 1 (M1), S2KP2, and weaving the carries. **2** When carrying yarn over several stitches, weave the carried yarn along the WS of the work. **3** Change to double-pointed needles (dpns) when necessary. **4** Instructions are given for Phoenix of Love (Woodland Fantasy, Grandma's Garden).

TAM
Ribbing
With smaller circular needle and Main Color (MC), cast on 61 (60, 60) stitches, using chain cast-on. Turn work.
Next row * K1, p1 into next stitch; repeat from *—122 (120, 120) stitches. Do not turn. Place marker and join, being careful not to twist stitches.
Round 1 * Slip (sl) 1 purlwise with yarn in back, k1; repeat from *.
Round 2 * K1, sl 1 purlwise with yarn in front; repeat from *.
Rounds 3 and 4 Repeat Rounds 1 and 2. Change to larger circular needle. Work k1, p1 rib for 1". Remove waste yarn from cast-on.

Sides
Increase Round * K2, M1; repeat from * (for Phoenix of Love, omit last M1)—182 (180, 180) stitches.
PHOENIX OF LOVE Work 13 rounds of Chart A. Knit 3 rounds with MC, increasing 2 stitches evenly around on last round—184 stitches. Work 7 rounds of Chart B. Knit 3 rounds with MC, decreasing 2 stitches evenly around on last round—182 stitches.
WOODLAND FANTASY Work 6 rounds of Chart A. Work 12 rounds of Chart B. Knit 3 rounds with MC. Work 6 rounds of Chart A. **Next round** * K13, k2tog; repeat from *— 168 stitches.
GRANDMA'S GARDEN Work 7 rounds of Chart A. Work 5 rounds of Chart B. Work 9 rounds of Chart C. Work Rounds 1–4 of Chart B. **Next round** With MC, * k7, k2tog; repeat from *—160 stitches. Work 7 rounds of Chart D. Work Rounds 1–4 of Chart B. **Next round** With MC, * k3, k2tog, [k1, (k2tog) twice] 15 times; repeat from * once more—98 stitches.

Wheel
Work 30 (25, 13) rounds of Chart C (C, E)—14 stitches.

JAMIESON'S 2-ply jumper weight Shetland wool in assorted colors

Phoenix of love

Colors used: garnet, strawberry, cream, white, slate blue

Chart C

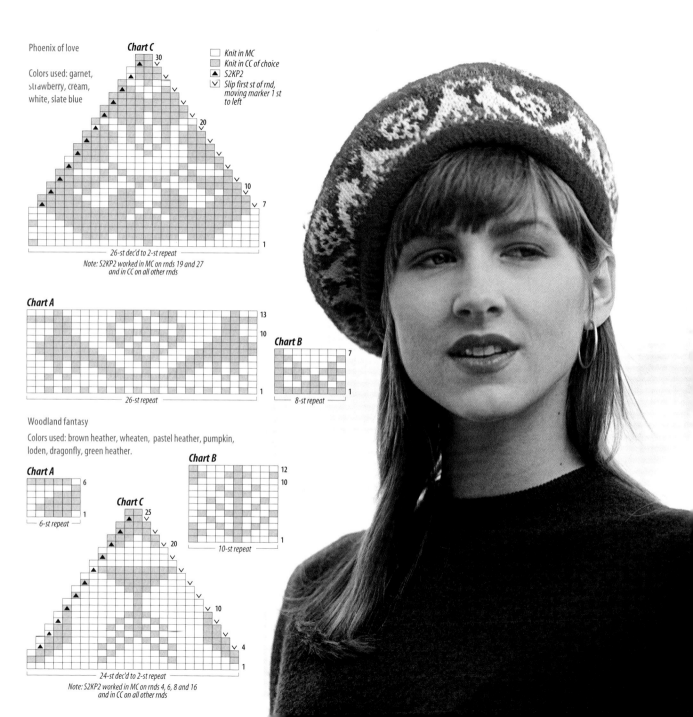

Knit in MC
Knit in CC of choice
▲ S2KP2
∨ Slip first st of rnd, moving marker 1 st to left

30

20

10

7

1

26-st dec'd to 2-st repeat

Note: S2KP2 worked in MC on rnds 19 and 27 and in CC on all other rnds

Chart A

13

10

1

26-st repeat

Chart B

7

1

8-st repeat

Woodland fantasy

Colors used: brown heather, wheaten, pastel heather, pumpkin, loden, dragonfly, green heather.

Chart A

6

1

6-st repeat

Chart B

12

10

1

10-st repeat

Chart C

25

20

10

4

1

24-st dec'd to 2-st repeat

Note: S2KP2 worked in MC on rnds 4, 6, 8 and 16 and in CC on all other rnds

Next round [K1, S2KP2] 3 times, k2tog—5 stitches.
Cut yarn, run tail through remaining stitches and pull tight.

Finishing
Wash gently by hand in warm water. Block by stretching and smoothing over desired shape. Allow to dry completely.

Grandma's Garden

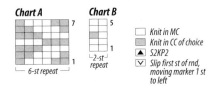

Chart A
7
6-st repeat
1

Chart B
5
2-st repeat
1

☐ Knit in MC
▨ Knit in CC of choice
▲ S2KP2
∨ Slip first st of rnd, moving marker 1 st to left

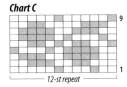

Chart C
9
12-st repeat
1

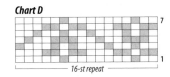

Chart D
7
16-st repeat
1

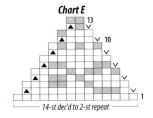

Chart E
13
10
1
14-st dec'd to 2-st repeat

21

This chapeau is fun-loving and fun knitting. It's sure to give you a with-it look. You can work a child's size, a medium adult size, or a larger hat simply by working at larger or smaller gauges.

Designed by Anna Zilboorg

Pentagon Power

INTERMEDIATE

One size
Circumference 20"

10cm/4"

22

20

• over chart pattern, using larger needles

1 2 3 **4** 5 6

• Medium weight
• A 150 yds
• B 90 yds
• C 90 yds

• 3.5mm/US4 and 4.5mm/US7, or size to
obtain gauge, 40cm/16" long

• four 4.5mm/US7

Notes

1 See *Techniques,* page 76, for make 1 (M1). **2** Change to double-pointed needles when necessary.

HAT

With smaller circular needle, cast on 100 stitches. Place marker and join, being careful not to twist stitches.
Begin Chart: Round 1 Work 20-stitch repeat 5 times.
Continue in chart pattern through Round 5. Change to larger circular needle. Work through chart Round 74—5 stitches remain. Cut yarn and pull through stitches.

Finishing

Steam top of hat over a rolled towel. Turn hat upside down and pin widest part in 5 points, making sides even. Steam hat, including lower edge.

Stitch key
☐ Knit   ⊟ Purl
☑ K2tog
▽ Sl 1 purlwise with yarn in back
Ⓜ M1
Ⓑ ***Make Bobble*** [K1, yo, k1, yo, k1] in one stitch, turn. K5, turn. P5, turn. K5, turn. With right needle, slip 2nd, 3rd, 4th, then 5th stitch on left needle over first stitch and off needle; knit remaining stitch (bobble complete).
▲ Slip last 2 sts of repeat together knitwise, k first st of next repeat, p2sso.

Color key
▨ Purple (A)
▨ Raspberry (B)
▨ Olive (C)

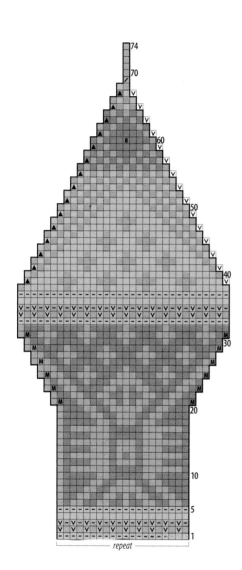

CLASSIC ELITE *Tapestry (wool, mohair; 50g; 95 yds) in 2279 Purple (A),
2234 Raspberry (B), 2238 Olive (C)*

65

This hat was designed to use up leftovers by working small Fair Isle charts with bands of garter stitch (worked as purl rounds). Each hat will be unique and a lot of fun to make. The bells add a jester-like appearance.

Designed by Cati Bourgeois Van Veen

Fabulous Funky Headgear

INTERMEDIATE

Child S (Adult M, L)
Circumference 19 (20½, 20½)"

10cm/4"

24 (20)
15 (14)
• over stockinette stitch
(knit every round)

1 2 3 4 **5** 6

• Bulky weight
CHILD • 185 yds assorted colors
ADULT M & L • 225 yds assorted colors

CHILD • 5.5mm/US9
ADULT • 6mm/US10
or size to obtain gauge
40cm/16" long and 60cm/24" long

&

• stitch markers
• 3 bells

Note

See *Techniques*, page 76, for 3-needle bind-off.

HAT

With 16" needle, cast on 72 stitches. Place marker (pm) and join, being careful not to twist stitches. Knit 12 (14, 16) rounds. Work Chart A (B, C), using colors desired, through round 16 (30, 27).

Shape top

Continue chart patterns, work as follows:
Next round K12, pm, [k24, pm] twice, k12. Continue in patterns, increase 1 stitch (working increases into pattern) before and after each of these 3 markers (6 stitches increased) every round 6 times—108 stitches. Change to 24" circular needle and continue to increase for 6 rounds more—144 stitches.
Next 2 rounds Continue patterns, increase 2 stitches before and after each marker—168 stitches. Work 1 round even, removing all but round marker. With bright color and using 3-needle bind-off, join 28 stitches after round marker together with 28 stitches before round marker for first point; then join

next 28 stitches together with following 28 stitches for 2nd point; join next 28 stitches together with last 28 stitches for 3rd point. Cut yarn and secure. Sew a bell on each point.

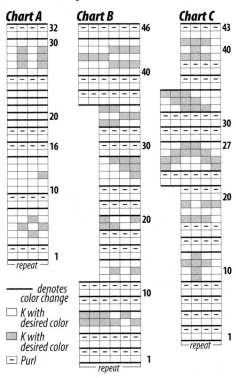

Chart A 32 30 20 16 10 1 *repeat*

Chart B 46 40 30 20 10 1 *repeat*

Chart C 43 40 30 27 20 10 1 *repeat*

—— denotes color change
☐ K with desired color
▨ K with desired color
⊟ Purl

PHILOSOPHER'S WOOL COMPANY 3 Ply
(wool; 112g; 150 yds) Assorted colors

23

INTERMEDIATE

One size
Circumference 21¼"

10cm/4"

28
26
• over Chart A, using larger needle

1 2 **3** 4 5 6
• Light weight
A • 125 yds
B • 125 yds

• 2.25mm/US1 and 3.5mm/US4, or size to
obtain gauge, 40cm/16" long

• four 3.5mm/US4

A chenille and a smooth wool add to the intricate rhythms of this color pattern. Small needles and a fine gauge give this hat firmness. Bogolanfini, the mud-dyed textiles of the Mali people, are made up of simple geometric shapes representing items of symbolic importance.

Designed by Nadia Severns

Fini Blues

Notes
1 See *Techniques*, page 76, for SK2P and SSK. *2* Change to double-pointed needles (dpn) when necessary.

HAT
With smaller needles and B, cast on 110 stitches. Place marker (pm) and join, being careful not to twist stitches. Work 6 rounds in k1, p1 rib. Change to larger needles. Knit 1 round, increasing 28 stitches evenly around—138 stitches. With A, knit 1 round. With B, knit 1 round. Work 20 rounds of Chart A. Knit 1 round with B, 1 round with A, 1 round with B.

Braid
Round 1 * K1B, k1A; repeat from *.
Round 2 Bring both colors to RS of work. * P1B, p1A; repeat from *, leaving yarns on RS and always bringing the new color up over the old color.
Round 3 * P1B, p1A; repeat from *, this time bring each color from under the old color. Return yarn to WS.
With B, knit 1 round, with A, knit 1 round.
Next round With B, * SSK, k21; repeat from *—132 stitches.

Shape crown
Work 24 rounds of Chart B—12 stitches. Cut yarn, leaving a long tail of B. Thread tail through stitches, draw together tightly and secure on WS.

Finishing
Block. Find something of the appropriate size and shape to block over (a straight-sided cookie tin or a cooking pot). Place hat on it and press firmly with a well dampened cloth. Allow to dry.

ROWAN Fine Cotton Chenille (cotton, polyester; 50g; 170 yds) 376 Ecru (A) and Designer DK Wool (wool; 50g; 125 yds) in 691/H Brown (B)

Chart A

20

10

1

23-st repeat

Color key
- A
- B

Stitch key
- Knit
- SK2P

Chart B

24

20

10

6

1

22-st repeat

"I have admired a striped hat photographed in Knitting in the Nordic Tradition for a long time. Starting with its pinstripes, I added braid and I-cord (magically knit-in while knitting around). Mittens must match, of course."

Designed by Sidna Farley

Pinstripes

INTERMEDIATE

One size
Head circumference 21"
Hand circumference 7½"

10cm/4"

23
19

• over Pinstripe Pattern

1 2 3 **4** 5 6

• Medium weight
HAT A & B • 90 yds each
C, D, E • 40 yds each
MITTENS A & B • 90 yds each
C, D, E • 40 yds each

• 5mm/US8, or size to obtain gauge,
40cm/16" long

• four 5mm/US8

&

• stitch markers

Notes

1 See *Techniques,* page 76, for Make 1 (M1), SSK, SK2P, I-cord, invisible cast-on and grafting. **2** Change to double-pointed needles (dpn) when necessary.

Pinstripe Pattern (over an even number of stitches)

(**Note** Always carry B over A on WS of work. The color that goes under is predominant on the front.)
Round 1 * K1A, k1B; repeat from *. Repeat Round 1 for Pinstripe Pattern.

Braid

Round 1 With A, knit.
Round 2 * K1A, k1C; repeat from * to last 2 stitches, k1A, bring yarn forward and drop it in the front, k1C and bring that yarn to the front.
Round 3 * Insert needle purlwise into A stitch, bring A yarn over C yarn and purl stitch on needle, then purl C stitch, bringing C yarn over A yarn; repeat from *, making sure to bring the yarn for the new stitch over the previous yarn.
Round 4 With A, knit.

HAT

With circular needle and A, cast on 96 stitches. Place marker and join, being careful not to twist stitches. Knit every round for 1". Work in Pinstripe Pattern for 2". Work 4 rounds of Braid.

I-cord

Next round * Work Pinstripe Pattern for 15 stitches (ending with an A stitch), join a length of C, approximately 6 yds long and [k1, yarn over (yo), k1] into next stitch; repeat from * 5 times more, replacing C with D, E, C, D, then E.
Next round * Work 15 stitches Pinstripe Pattern, bring I-cord yarn up from under A and B, and knit 3 I-cord stitches; repeat from *. Continue I-cord and Pinstripe Pattern until piece measures 3½" above Braid.

Shape crown

Decrease round * SSK with A, work in pattern as established to 2 stitches before I-cord, k2tog with A, work I-cord; repeat from *. Work 1 round even, matching colors. Repeat last 2 rounds until 3 pinstripe stitches remain in each section.
Next round * SK2P with A, then work I-cord

BROWN SHEEP Top of the Lamb single ply worsted (wool; 115g; 190 yds) in 210 Onyx (A), 101 Stone (B), 235 Terra Cotta (C), 331 Mallard (D), and 201 Brick Red (E)

as established; repeat from *. Bring I-cord yarns to outside, break off A and B, pull tail of A yarn through 6 A stitches. Work I-cords separately for 4½–5". Cut yarn and pull each tail through its remaining stitches. With A, wrap I-cords together tightly at top of hat. Starting at tip of one I-cord, sew it into a spiral. Repeat with every other cord (one spiral of each color). Sew each remaining I-cord into center to form a loop.

Finishing
Sew cast-on edge to inside along bumps left by Round 4 of Braid.

LEFT MITTEN
Hand
With dpns and A, cast on 36 stitches, using invisible cast-on, turn, knit 1 row onto 3 dpns, join, being careful not to twist stitches. Work in Pinstripe Pattern for 8 rounds.

Work braid
Work Rounds 1–3 of Braid. **Next round** With A, k5, * M1, k9; repeat from * to last 4 stitches, M1, k4—40 stitches.
Next round Work 13 stitches in Pinstripe Pattern (ending with A), join a length of C approximately 2½ yards long and knit into front and back of next stitch (this establishes a 2-stitch I-cord, which isn't as bulky as a 3-stitch cord and therefore better for mittens), place marker (pm), k1A, k1B, k1A (thumb gusset), work another 2-stitch I-cord with D, k1A, work another 2-stitch I-cord with E, work 19 stitches in Pinstripe Pattern, work a 2-stitch I-cord with E. Work 3 rounds in pattern as established. Work 12 rounds in patterns as established, work Thumb Gusset Chart between markers.
Next round Work across palm to first C I-cord, slip (sl) next 11 stitches onto waste yarn (removing markers), with A, loop cast on 5 stitches, catching B in back; join to other side and complete round.
Next round Re-establish pinstripe over 5 cast-on stitches.

Work even for 5½" or just short of top of little finger.
Decrease round * SSK with A, work to 2 stitches before I-cord, k2tog with A, work I-cord; repeat from *. Work 1 round even. Repeat Decrease Round every round until 3 stitches remain between I-cords.
Next round [With A, SK2P, work I-cord] twice. Graft the 2 sides of I-cord together, catching remaining A stitch on side.

Thumb
With dpn, work across held stitches, M1 A stitch between thumb and palm I-cords, pick up and knit [1B, 1A] twice, 1B along cast-on stitches making sure only A shows on the cast-on side; M1 A stitch in A stitch at other side of thumb—18 stitches. Join. Work even in Pinstripe and I-cord pattern as established for 2¾" (or ½" short of top of thumb). Then decrease every round as before, and graft I-cord stitches together.

Finishing
3-stitch I-cord bottom border
Place 36 cast-on stitches on needle, removing waste yarn. With D, invisibly cast on 3 stitches, * k2, SSK (3rd stitch with next border stitch); repeat from *. Graft beginning to end.

RIGHT MITTEN
Hand
Work as for Left Mitten through Braid.
Next round Work 19 stitches in Pinstripe Pattern (ending with an A stitch), work 2-stitch I-cord with E, k1A, 2-stitch I-cord with D, pm, k1A, k1B, k1A (thumb gusset), pm, 2-stitch I-cord with D, 13 stitches in Pinstripe Pattern, 2-stitch I-cord with E. Continue as for Left Mitten.

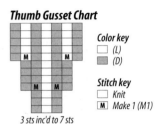

Thumb Gusset Chart

Color key
☐ (L)
▨ (D)

Stitch key
☐ Knit
M Make 1 (M1)

3 sts inc'd to 7 sts

Knitted hats travel well, folded in a pocket or purse until needed. Everybody needs such a hat. Beyond the obvious—keeping the wearer warm and dry on cold, wet days—they conquer the gloom of winter with their color and pattern, their balls and bobbles. They brighten the day for both wearer and watcher.

Designed by Anna Zilboorg

Spire Hat

INTERMEDIATE

One size (fits children and most adults)

10cm/4"

22

20

• over stockinette stitch (knit all rounds) with larger needles

1 2 3 **4** 5 6

• Medium weight
MC, CC1 • 80 yds each
CC2 & CC3 • 60 yds each

• 3.75mm/US5 and 4.5mm/US7 or size to obtain gauge, 40cm/16" long

• 3.75mm/US5 and 4.5mm/US7

&

• stitch marker
• tapestry needle

Notes
1 See *Techniques*, page 76, for SSK, S2KP2, lifted increase, and M1. **2** On Rows 9 and 17 of Chart B there are long carries. Catch the pattern color over the pattern stitches on the preceding row; this way, no color shows through. **3** Slip (sl) stitches purlwise with yarn at WS of work. **4** Change to double-pointed needles (dpn) when necessary.

HAT
With smaller circular needle and MC, cast on 96 stitches, join, being careful not to twist stitches.

Work border
Round 1 With MC, purl.
Round 2 With CC3, * k1, sl 1; repeat from *.
Round 3 With CC3, * p1, sl 1; repeat from *.
Round 4 With MC, knit.
Round 5 With MC, purl.
Change to larger needle. Work 14 rounds of Chart A—144 stitches. Knit 1 round with MC. Repeat 5-round border. Work 36 rounds of Chart B—16 stitches.

Ball on top
Change to smaller dpn. With CC1, k2tog around—8 stitches remain.
Round 1 Knit.
Round 2 * K1, M1; repeat from *—16 stitches.
Round 3 Knit.
Round 4 * K2, M1; repeat from *—24 stitches.
Round 5 Knit.
Round 6 * K2tog; repeat from *—12 stitches.
Round 7 Knit.
Make a small tight ball of yarn and stuff it into the knitting.
Round 8 * K2tog; repeat from *—6 stitches.
Cut a tail of yarn several inches long. Thread it in a needle and through the remaining stitches twice. Pull tight. Push the needle through the ball and out the base of the ball. Wrap yarn 4 or 5 times around, then push needle under the wraps and up through the ball. Pull tight and cut yarn close to the ball.

Worsted weight wool in Black
(MC), Red (CC1), Purple
(CC2), and Gold (CC3)

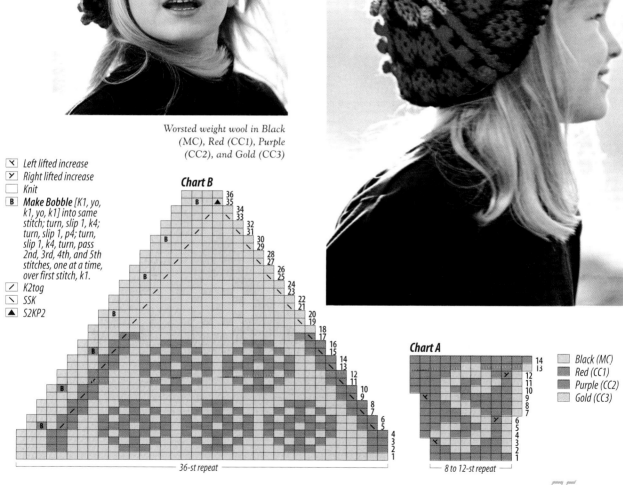

⊠	Left lifted increase
⊻	Right lifted increase
□	Knit
B	**Make Bobble** [K1, yo, k1, yo, k1] into same stitch; turn, slip 1, k4; turn, slip 1, p4; turn, slip 1, k4, turn, pass 2nd, 3rd, 4th, and 5th stitches, one at a time, over first stitch, k1.
╱	K2tog
╲	SSK
▲	S2KP2

Chart B

36-st repeat

Chart A

8 to 12-st repeat

☐	Black (MC)
☐	Red (CC1)
☐	Purple (CC2)
☐	Gold (CC3)

75

KNIT CAST-ON

1 Start with a slipknot on left needle (first cast-on stitch). Insert right needle into slipknot from front. Wrap yarn over right needle as if to knit.

2 Bring yarn through slipknot, forming a loop on right needle.
3 Insert left needle **under** loop and slip loop off right needle. One additional stitch cast on.

4 Insert right needle into the last stitch on left needle as if to knit. Knit a stitch and transfer it to the left needle as in Step 3. Repeat Step 4 for each additional stitch.

CROCHET CAST-ON

1 Leaving a short tail, make a slipknot on crochet hook. Hold hook in right hand; in left hand, hold knitting needle on top of yarn and behind hook. With hook to left of yarn, bring yarn through loop on hook; yarn goes over top of needle, forming a stitch.

2 Bring yarn under point of needle and hook yarn through loop forming next stitch. Repeat Step 2 until 1 stitch remains to cast on. Slip loop from hook to needle for last stitch.

LOOP CAST-ON (ALSO CALLED E-WRAP CAST-ON)

Often used to cast on a few stitches, as for a buttonhole
1 Hold needle and tail in left hand.
2 Bring right index finger under yarn, pointing toward you.

3 Turn index finger to point away from you.
4 Insert tip of needle under yarn on index finger (see above); remove finger and draw yarn snug, forming a stitch.
Repeat Steps 2–4 until all stitches are on needle.

INVISIBLE CAST-ON

A temporary cast-on

1 Knot working yarn to contrasting waste yarn. Hold needle and knot in right hand. Tension both strands in left hand; separate strands so waste yarn is over index finger, working yarn over thumb. Bring needle between strands and under thumb yarn so working yarn forms a yarn-over in front of waste yarn.

2 Holding both yarns taut, pivot hand toward you, bringing working yarn under and behind waste yarn. Bring needle behind and under working yarn so working yarn forms a yarn-over behind waste yarn.

3 Pivot hand away from you, bringing working yarn under and in front of waste yarn. Bring needle between strands and under working yarn, forming a yarn-over in front of waste yarn. Each yarn-over forms a stitch.

Repeat Steps 2–3 for required number of stitches. For an even number, twist working yarn around waste strand before knitting the first row.

CHAIN CAST-ON

A temporary cast-on

1 With crochet hook and waste yarn, loosely chain the number of stitches needed, plus a few extra chains. Cut yarn.
2 With needle and main yarn, pick up and knit 1 stitch into the back 'purl bump' of the first

chain. Continue, knitting 1 stitch into each chain until you have the required number of stitches. Do not work into remaining chains.

CROCHET CHAIN STITCH (ch st, ch)

1 Make a slipknot to begin.
2 Catch yarn and draw through loop on hook.

First chain made. Repeat Step 2.

ELONGATED STITCH

1 Knit 1, EXCEPT wrap yarn 2 or more times around needle, instead of once, before drawing new stitch through old stitch.

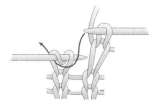

2 On next row, knit the stitch, dropping extra wrap(s) as stitch is pulled off left needle.

ABBREVIATIONS

CC contrasting color
cn cable needle
cm centimeter(s)
dec decreas(e)(ed)(es)(ing)
dpn double-pointed needle(s)
g gram(s)
" inch(es)
inc increas(e)(ed)(es)(ing)
k knit(ting)(s)(ted)
LH left-hand
M1 Make one stitch (increase)
m meter(s)
mm millimeter(s)
MC main color
oz ounce(s)
p purl(ed)(ing)(s) or page
pm place marker
psso pass slipped stitch(es) over
RH right-hand
RS right side(s)
sc single crochet
sl slip(ped)(ping)
SKP slip, knit, psso
SSK slip, slip, knit these 2 sts tog
SSP slip, slip, purl these 2 sts tog
st(s) stitch(es)
St st stockinette stitch
tbl through back of loop(s)
WS wrong side(s)
wyib with yarn in back
wyif with yarn in front
yd(s) yard(s)
yo(2) yarn over (twice)

TUBULAR CAST-ON

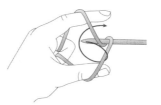

1 Leaving a tail approximately 4 times the width of the cast-on, fold the yarn over a needle 3–4 sizes smaller than main needle (1–2 sizes smaller than ribbing needle). Bring yarn between fingers of left hand and wrap around little finger as shown.

2 Bring left thumb and index finger between strands, arranging so tail is on thumb side. Open thumb and finger so strands form a diamond. Take needle **over index yarn, then under it.**

3 Bring needle **over thumb yarn** then **under it and under index yarn,** forming a purl stitch on needle.

4 Bring needle toward you, **over thumb yarn, under it,** and up between the two yarns.

5 Bring needle **over and under** the **index yarn**. Bring index yarn **under thumb yarn,** forming a knit stitch on the needle.

6 Take needle over index yarn, then under it. Repeat Steps 3–6.

7 End with Step 3. Note that knit stitches alternate with purl stitches.

8 Work 2 rows double knit as follows: **Row 1** * Knit 1 in back loop, slip 1 purlwise with yarn in front; repeat from *.
Row 2 * Knit 1, slip 1 purlwise with yarn in front; repeat from *.
9 Change to larger needles and work knit 1, purl 1 rib or repeat Row 2 for double-knit fabric.

BACKWARD SINGLE CROCHET, CRAB STITCH

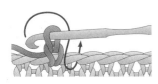

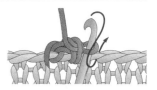

1 Insert hook into a stitch, catch yarn, and pull up a loop. Catch yarn and pull a loop through the loop on the hook.
2 Insert hook into next stitch to right.

3 Catch yarn and pull through stitch only (as shown). As soon as hook clears the stitch, flip your wrist (and the hook). There are 2 loops on the hook, and the just-made loop is to the front of the hook (left of the old loop).

4 Catch yarn and pull through both loops on hook; 1 backward single crochet completed.

5 Continue working to the right, repeating Steps 2–4.

3-NEEDLE BIND-OFF

Bind-off ridge on wrong side
1 With stitches on 2 needles, place ***right sides together***.
* Knit 2 stitches together (1 from front needle and 1 from back needle); repeat from * once more (as shown).
2 With left needle, pass first stitch on right needle over second stitch and off right needle.

3 Knit next 2 stitches together.
4 Repeat Step 2.
5 Repeat Steps 3 and 4, end by drawing yarn through last stitch.

Bind-off ridge on right side
Work as for ridge on wrong side, EXCEPT, with ***wrong sides together***.

SINGLE CROCHET (sc)

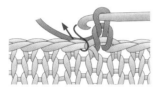  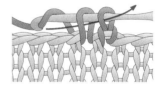

1 Insert hook into a stitch, catch yarn, and pull up a loop. Catch yarn and pull through the loop on the hook.
2 Insert hook into next stitch to the left.

3 Catch yarn and pull through the stitch; 2 loops on hook.

4 Catch yarn and pull through both loops on hook; 1 single crochet completed. Repeat Steps 2–4.

SHORT ROWS

Each short row adds 2 rows of knitting across a section of the work. Since the work is turned before completing a row, stitches must be wrapped at the turn to prevent holes. Wrap and turn as follows:

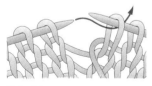 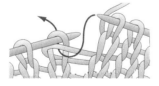  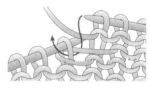

Knit side
1 With yarn in back, slip next stitch as if to purl. Bring yarn to front of work and slip stitch back to left needle (as shown). Turn work.
2 With yarn in front, slip next stitch as if to purl. Work to end.

3 When you come to the wrap on a following knit row, hide the wrap by knitting it together with the stitch it wraps.

Purl side
1 With yarn in front, slip next stitch as if to purl. Bring yarn to back of work and slip stitch back to left needle (as shown). Turn work.
2 With yarn in back, slip next stitch as if to purl. Work to end.

3 When you come to the wrap on a following purl row, hide the wrap by purling it together with the stitch it wraps.

PICK UP AND KNIT

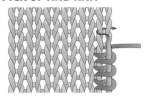

Insert needle in space **between** first and second stitches, catch yarn and knit a stitch.

KNIT, PURL THROUGH BACK LOOP (k1 tbl, p1 tbl)

1 With right needle behind left needle and right leg of stitch, insert needle into stitch…

2 …and **knit**.

Or, with right needle behind left needle, insert right needle into stitch from left to right and **purl**.

KNIT INTO FRONT AND BACK (kf&b)

1 Knit into the front of next stitch on left needle, but do not pull the stitch off the needle.
2 Take right needle to back, then knit through the back of the same stitch.

3 Pull stitch off left needle. Completed increase: 2 stitches from 1 stitch. This increase results in a purl bump after the knit stitch.

SLIP PURLWISE (sl 1 p-wise)

1 Insert right needle into next stitch on left needle from back to front (as if to purl).

2 Slide stitch from left to right needle. Stitch orientation does not change (right leg of stitch loop is at front of needle).

MAKE 1 LEFT (M1L), KNIT

Insert left needle from front to back under strand between last stitch knitted and first stitch on left needle. Knit, twisting strand by working into loop at back of needle.

Completed M1L knit: a left-slanting increase.

MAKE 1 RIGHT (M1R), KNIT

Insert left needle from back to front under strand between last stitch knitted and first stitch on left needle. Knit, twisting the strand by working into loop at front of the needle.

Completed M1R knit: a right-slanting increase.

80

SLIP KNITWISE (sl 1 k-wise)

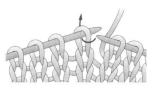

1 Insert right needle into next stitch on left needle from front to back (as if to knit).

2 Slide stitch from left to right needle. Stitch orientation changes (right leg of stitch loop is at back of needle).

The stitch slipped knitwise can be a knit or a purl.

SK2P, sl 1-k2tog-psso

1 Slip 1 stitch knitwise.
2 Knit next 2 stitches together.
3 Pass the slipped stitch over the k2tog: 3 stitches become 1; the right stitch is on top.
The result is a left-slanting double decrease.

SSK

1 Slip 2 stitches *separately* to right needle as if to knit.

2 Slip left needle into these 2 stitches from left to right and knit them together: 2 stitches become 1.

The result is a left-slanting decrease.

S2KP2, sl 2-k1-p2sso

1 Slip 2 stitches *together* to right needle as if to knit.

2 Knit next stitch.

3 Pass 2 slipped stitches over knit stitch and off right needle: 3 stitches become 1; the center stitch is on top.

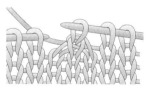

The result is a centered double decrease.

POMPONS

1 Cut 2 pieces of cardboard half the desired width of the pompon.
2 Place a length of yarn between cardboard pieces.
3 Hold the pieces together and wrap yarn around them.

4 Tie the length of yarn tightly at one edge.
5 Cut the wrapped yarn on opposite side.

6 Remove cardboard, fluff, and trim pompon.
7 Use ties to attach.

I-CORD

Make a tiny tube of stockinette stitch with 2 double-pointed needles:
1 Cast on 3 or 4 sts.
2 Knit. Do not turn work. Slide stitches to opposite end of needle. Repeat Step 2 until cord is the desired length.

TASSELS

1 Wrap yarn around a piece of cardboard that is the desired length of the tassel. Thread a strand of yarn under the wraps, and tie it at the top, leaving a long end.

2 Cut the wrapped yarn at lower edge. Wrap the long end of yarn around upper edge and thread the yarn through the top as shown. Trim strands.

TWISTED CORD

1 Cut strands 6 times the length of cord needed. Fold in half and knot cut ends together.
2 Place knotted end over a door knob or hook and right index finger in folded end, then twist cord tightly.

3 Fold cord in half, smoothing as it twists on itself. Pull knot through original fold to secure.

SSP

Use instead of p2tog-tbl to avoid twisting the stitches.

1 Slip 2 stitches **separately** to right needle as if to knit.

2 Slip these 2 stitches back onto left needle. Insert right needle through their 'back loops,' into the second stitch and then the first.

3 Purl them together: 2 stitches become 1.

The result is a left-slanting decrease.

YARN-OVER (yo)

Between knit stitches
Bring yarn under needle to the front, take it over the needle to the back and knit the next stitch.

Completed yo increase.

After a knit, before a purl
Bring yarn under the needle to the front, over the needle to the back, then under the needle to the front; purl next stitch.

After a purl, before a knit
With yarn in front of the needle, bring it over the needle to the back; knit next stitch.

GRAFT IN GARTER

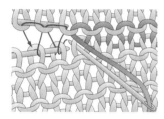

1 Arrange stitches on 2 needles so stitches on lower, or front, needle come out of purl bumps and stitches on the upper, or back, needle come out of smooth knits.
2 Thread a blunt needle with matching yarn (approximately 1" per stitch).
3 Working from right to left, begin with Steps 3a and 3b:
3a **Front needle:** bring yarn through first stitch **as if to purl,** leave stitch **on needle.**
3b **Back needle:** repeat Step 3a.
4a **Front needle:** bring yarn through first stitch **as if to knit, slip off** needle; through next stitch **as if to purl, leave on** needle.
4b **Back needle:** repeat Step 4a. Repeat Steps 4a and 4b until 1 stitch remains on each needle.
5a **Front needle:** bring yarn through stitch **as if to knit,** slip **off needle.**
5b **Back needle:** repeat Step 5a.
6 Adjust tension to match rest of knitting.

GRAFT IN STOCKINETTE

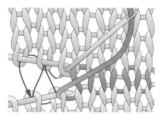

1 Arrange stitches on 2 needles as shown.
2 Thread a blunt needle with matching yarn (approximately 1" per stitch).
3 Working from right to left, with right sides facing you, begin with Steps 3a and 3b:
3a **Front needle:** bring yarn through first stitch **as if to purl,** leave stitch **on needle.**
3b **Back needle:** bring yarn through first stitch **as if to knit,** leave stitch **on needle.**
4a **Front needle:** bring yarn through first stitch **as if to knit, slip off** needle; through next stitch **as if to purl,** leave stitch **on needle.**
4b **Back needle:** bring yarn through first stitch **as if to purl, slip off** needle; through next stitch **as if to knit,** leave stitch **on needle.**
Repeat Steps 4a and 4b until 1 stitch remains on each needle.
5a **Front needle:** bring yarn through stitch **as if to knit,** slip **off needle.**
5b **Back needle:** bring yarn through stitch **as if to purl,** slip **off needle.**
6 Adjust tension to match rest of knitting.

KNITTING IN ROUNDS

• After casting on, do not turn work. Knit into first cast-on stitch to join. Stop. Check to make sure that the cast-on does not spiral around the needle. If it does, undo the stitch, remove the spiral, then rejoin.
• Check your knitting at end of first and second rounds and make sure you have no twists.
• Mark the beginning of a round in one of three ways:
1 Place a marker on needle.
2 Use a safety pin in the fabric.
3 Weave your leftover cast-on tail between first and last stitch of round.

WORKING WITH 3 DOUBLE-POINTED NEEDLES (DPNS)

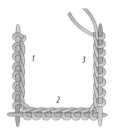
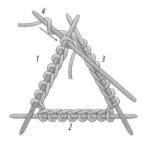

Cast stitches onto 1 dpn.
1 Rearrange stitches on 3 dpns. Check carefully that stitches are not twisted around a dpn or between dpns before beginning to work in rounds.

2 With a 4th dpn, work all stitches from first dpn. Use that empty dpn to work the stitches from the 2nd dpn. Use that empty dpn to work the stitches from the 3rd dpn—one round completed.

Place a marker between first and second stitch of first needle to mark beginning of round.
Notice that you work with only 2 dpns at a time. As you work the first few rounds, be careful that the stitches do not twist between the needles.

WORKING WITH 4 DOUBLE-POINTED NEEDLES (DPNS)

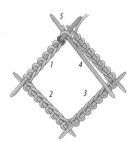

If instructions recommend working with a set of 5 dpns, arrange the stitches on 4 needles and knit with the fifth.

STRANDED 2-COLOR KNITTING

Two colors worked across a row form a color pattern: the unused color is carried (**stranded**) along the wrong side of the fabric. These 'carries' should not exceed 1 inch. **Weave** any carry longer than 1 inch along the wrong side.

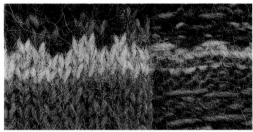

Right-side and wrong-side of stranded 2-color knitting.

TIPS
• Stranded knitting can be worked back and forth (flat) or in the round.
• Carries should not be too tight or too loose so as not to affect the gauge or distort the fabric.
• Never twist colors between color changes in stranded knitting.
• Fair Isle is a style of stranded knitting.

WEAVING THE CARRIES

The carried yarn is woven alternately above and below the working yarn on the purl side of the work. Weaving the carries results in a firmer fabric than stranding does.

From the knit side
To weave the carry above a knit stitch: Insert needle into stitch and under woven yarn, then knit the stitch as usual.

To weave the carry below a knit stitch: Insert needle into stitch and over woven yarn, then knit the stitch as usual.

From the purl side
To weave the carry above a purl stitch: Insert needle into stitch and under woven yarn, then purl the stitch as usual.

To weave the carry below a purl stitch: Insert needle into stitch and over woven yarn, then purl the stitch as usual.

DUPLICATE STITCH

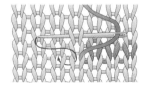

Duplicate stitch (also known as **swiss darning**) is just that: with a blunt tapestry needle threaded with a length of yarn of a contrasting color, cover a knitted stitch with an embroidered stitch.

TIP
Duplicate stitch is perfect for:
• small color accents
• lines of color
• correcting mistakes

85

Specifications:

Conversion chart

centimeters		0.394	inches
grams		0.035	ounces
inches	X	2.54	centimeters
ounces		28.6	grams
meters		1.1	yards
yards		.91	meters

INTERMEDIATE
One size
Circumference 19"

Skill level
Size
  and measurements

10cm/4"

27

21

• over stockinette stitch
(knit on RS, purl on WS)

Gauge
  *The number of stitches and
  rows you need in 10 cm or
  4", worked as specified.*

1 2 3 **4** 5 6

• Medium weight
MC, A, B, C, D, E, F • 88 yds each

Yarn weight
  and amount in yards

• four 4.5mm/US7 double-pointed needles
(dpn), or size to obtain gauge

Type of needles
  *Straight, unless circular
  or double-pointed
  are recommended.*

• 4.5mm/US7
40cm/16" long

Any extras

&

• stitch marker
• yarn needle

Needles/Hooks

US	MM	HOOK
0	2	A
1	2.25	B
2	2.75	C
3	3.25	D
4	3.5	E
5	3.75	F
6	4	G
7	4.5	7
8	5	H
9	5.5	I
10	6	J
10½	6.5	K
11	8	L
13	9	M
15	10	N
17	12.75	

Equivalent weights

¾	oz	20 g
1	oz	28 g
1½	oz	40 g
1¾	oz	50 g
2	oz	60 g
3½	oz	100 g

At a Glance

Yarn substitutions

Throughout this book, the photo caption describes the yarns and colors in the photograph. If a yarn is not available, its yardage and content information will help in making a substitution. Locate the Yarn Weight and Stockinette Stitch Gauge Range over 10cm to 4" on the chart. Compare that range with the information on the yarn label to find an appropriate yarn. These are guidelines only for commonly used gauges and needle sizes in specific yarn categories.

Measuring Gauge

10cm/4"

24 ▦ *GET GAUGE!*

18
• *over pattern stitch*
• *after blocking*

• Cast on a minimum of 5" worth of stitches.
• Work 2 rows of *knit*, continue to work in pattern specified for 5", then work 2 rows of knit.
Measure the swatch
• Steam or wash the swatch as you will the hat; after drying, measure the swatch, then count the stitches and the rows in 4".
• If your stitches number less than the pattern's, your stitches are too large and you should try a swatch with a smaller-sized needle.
• If your stitches number more than the pattern's, your stitches are too small and you should try a swatch with a larger-sized needle.
• If your rows number 1 or 2 less than the pattern's, try a swatch with the next smaller-sized needle. This may give you the correct row gauge without affecting the stitch gauge.
• If your rows number 1 or 2 more than the pattern's, try a swatch with the next larger-sized needle. This may give you the correct row gauge without affecting the stitch gauge.

TIP
Even if your gauge swatch is correct, don't stop measuring. Periodically measure the piece you are working on. Your gauge can change as you are working.

Yarn weight categories

Yarn Weight

1	2	3	4	5	6
Super Fine	**Fine**	**Light**	**Medium**	**Bulky**	**Super Bulky**

Also called

Sock Fingering Baby	Sport Baby	DK Light-Worsted	Worsted Afghan Aran	Chunky Craft Rug	Bulky Roving

Stockinette Stitch Gauge Range 10cm/4 inches

27 sts to 32 sts	23 sts to 26 sts	21 sts to 24 sts	16 sts to 20 sts	12 sts to 15 sts	6 sts to 11 sts

Recommended needle (metric)

2.25 mm to 3.25 mm	3.25 mm to 3.75 mm	3.75 mm to 4.5 mm	4.5 mm to 5.5 mm	5.5 mm to 8 mm	8 mm and larger

Recommended needle (US)

1 to 3	3 to 5	5 to 7	7 to 9	9 to 11	11 and larger

ENJOY

The online home of XRX Books,
Knitter's Magazine, and Stitches Events

www.knittinguniverse.com

EXPLORE

Knitter's thumb-through

Did you know you could thumb through
the pages of XRX Books? **Knitter's
thumb-through** is the online answer to
"try before you buy!"

Knitter's thumb-through

INTERACT

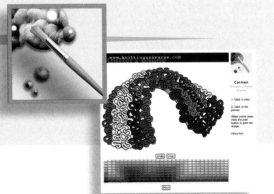

Knitter's Paint Box

Have you dabbled in digital paint? Work
out the available patterns any way you like,
then print the results.

- the Knitter's dozen series...

Contributors

Jane Davis

Maggie DeCuir

Susan Douglas

Maureen Egan Emlet

Sidna Farley

Sue Flanders

Julie Gaddy

Susan Guagliumi

Jean Inda

Rachel Nash Law

Maureen Mason-Jamieson

Angela Juergens

Cati Bourgeois Van Veen

Annie Modesitt

Betty Monroe

Deborah Newton

Penny Ollman

Gayle Roehm

Mary Rowe

Nadia Severns

Michele Woodford

David Xenakis

Lois Young

Anna Zilboorg